ANCIENT CULTURE AND SOCIETY

WAR IN THE ANCIENT WORLD
A SOCIAL HISTORY

ANCIENT CULTURE AND SOCIETY

General Editor
M. I. FINLEY
*Professor of Ancient History
in the University of Cambridge*

WAR IN THE
ANCIENT WORLD
A SOCIAL HISTORY

YVON GARLAN
Professor of Ancient History,
University of Rennes

Translated from the French by
JANET LLOYD

W · W · NORTON & COMPANY · INC · NEW YORK

Translation Copyright © 1975 by Chatto & Windus

First published as ''La Guerre dans l'Antiquité''
Copyright 1972 by Yvon Garlan and Fernand Nathan

Library of Congress Cataloging in Publication Data

Garlan, Yvon.
  War in the ancient world.

  (Ancient culture and society)
  Translation of La Guerre dans l'Antiquité.
  Bibliography: p.
  Includes index.
    1. Military art and science—History. 2. Greece—
Military antiquities. 3. Rome—Military antiquities.
I. Title.
U33.G3513   355'.00938   75-20463
ISBN 0-393-05566-3

                    Printed in the United States of America

            1   2   3   4   5   6   7   8   9

CONTENTS

ACKNOWLEDGEMENTS

The author and publishers are grateful to the following for permission to quote from copyright material:

J. M. Dent and Sons Ltd, and E. P. Dutton and Co Inc., for Livy's 'History of Rome' translated by W. M. Roberts.

William Heinemann Ltd and Harvard University Press for extracts from the works of Xenophon translated by C. L. Brownson (in The Loeb Classical Library) and extracts from the works of Dionysius of Halicarnassus translated by Earnest Cary (in The Loeb Classical Library).

Chronological Table

Preface

This is a slightly modified version of my book entitled *La guerre dans l'antiquité,* published in Paris in 1972. I have omitted the notes following the text, supplemented the bibliography and adapted it to English-speaking readers and, especially, made the chapters concerning the juridical aspects of war and modes of combat less technical.

I did the major work in Cambridge during the last quarter of 1971 while I was a Visiting Fellow of University (now Wolfson) College.

I should like to express my warmest thanks to Mrs Janet Lloyd for having devoted so much care to this translation and, above all, to my friend Moses Finley for his advice and comments which have contributed so much to the final version of this text.

Y.G.

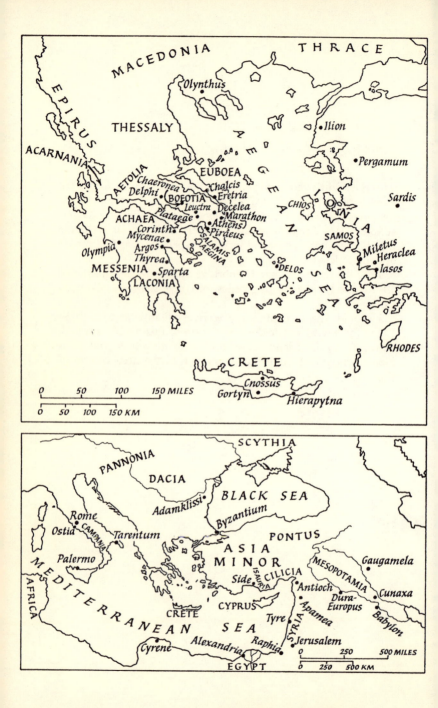

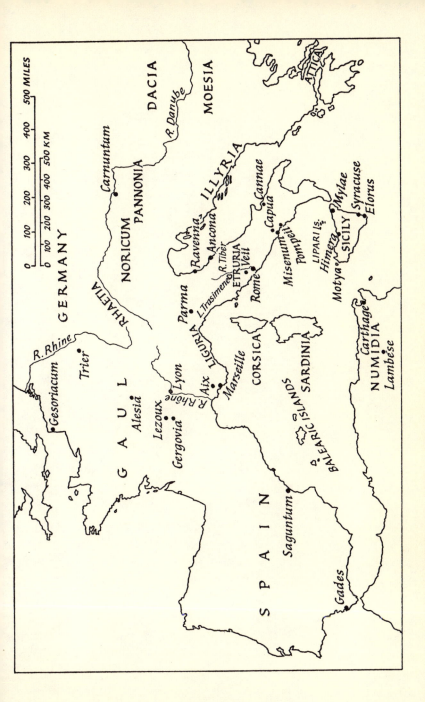

Introduction

Warfare in Ancient Societies

It is a commonplace to note the frequency of war in ancient societies, and in particular in the Greek and Roman worlds which are the subject of this study. Athens, for example, during the century and a half from the Persian wars (490 and 480–479 BC) to the battle of Chaeronea (338 BC) was at war, on average, more than two years out of every three, and never enjoyed a period of peace for as long as ten consecutive years. During the whole of Roman history down to the Empire the temple of Janus which 'signified when open that Rome had taken up arms, and when closed that peace reigned all about her' was, according to Livy (I, 19, 2–3) closed only on two occasions from the time of Numa Pompilius (beginning of the seventh century) to that of Augustus (end of the first century BC):

> Once after the first Punic war in the consulship of Titus Manlius, the second time, which heaven has allowed our generation to witness, after the battle of Actium, when peace on land and sea was secured by the emperor Caesar Augustus.

The '*pax Romana*', which the official propaganda of the Empire made so much of, seems to have been largely a myth; it took no account of the latent or declared hostilities which throughout several centuries kept an army of between three and five hundred thousand men constantly on a war footing. No doubt not all ancient states had such a warlike fate, but what is important is that this was the fate of those states that were in the vanguard of historical evolution.

The predominance of military affairs in ancient societies is also demonstrated by the dominating place which they hold in our documentation. In the first place they fostered the work of historians (to the tune of four fifths of it, in Toynbee's opinion). In some cases war provides the unifying theme—the Persian wars in Herodotus, the Peloponnesian War in Thucydides, Roman imperialism in Polybius; in others it rather provides the rhythm for the unfolding of a more wide-ranging account in the manner of a chronicle (as in Diodorus Siculus or Livy). Without wars the task of the historian, according to Tacitus (*Annals*, IV, 32), becomes difficult:

> I am aware that much of what I have described, and shall describe, may seem unimportant and trivial. But my chronicle is quite a different matter from histories of early Rome. Their subjects were great wars, cities stormed, kings routed and captured. Or if home affairs were their choice, they could turn freely to conflicts of consuls with tribunes, to land-and-corn laws, feuds of conservatives and commons. Mine, on the other hand, is a circumscribed, inglorious field. Peace was scarcely broken—if at all. Rome was plunged in gloom, the ruler uninterested in expanding the empire.

War also looms large in the philosophical, rhetorical and poetical writing of the ancients—not to mention the technical treatises of the Hellenistic and Roman periods which are specifically devoted to it. And the same can often be said of the epigraphical and archaeological evidence: thus, in architecture, quantitatively speaking the ancients appear to us principally as builders of fortifications.

Given these conditions, one would expect them to have considered war as a problem; one would have expected war to have forced them to think about its causes and its effects, to have been the principal subject for historical reflection. But this was far from the case.

True, Homer is aware of the diversity of motives which gave rise to the murderous whirlwind of Ares. Herodotus traces, in a more or less distant past, in the East as well as in the Greek world, the accumulation of grievances which led to the Persian wars; Thucydides introduces a new distinction between the superficial and the deeper causes of the conflict between Sparta and Athens, and discovers the conception of power politics. Polybius goes even further in taking into account causes and

16

pretexts as well as the actual opening of military hostilities. It is true too, that such philosophers as Plato, Aristotle and Cicero examine the nature of man in order to detect the fundamental cause of the continuous and pitiless rivalry which arrayed city against city and individual against individual. Nevertheless, all these 'explanations' attain only a low level of theoretical elaboration: they are too varied or too simple, too general or else too vague. They seem to float on the surface of the facts, because they never consider the phenomenon of war directly and in its entirety, taking into account its specific circumstances, its universality and also its diversity. In that they failed to go further in their analysis than a description of the underlying causes of particular wars or a mere condemnation of the perversity of human nature, the ancients were unable to treat war as a subject in itself. It is significant, in this respect, that war never provided the title or subject of a single ancient philosophical treatise.

Like war, peace too failed to acquire any true conceptual autonomy in antiquity. It was not that the ancients failed in practice to assess its advantages or to enjoy its delights, for war was seldom considered an absolute good, or a necessary evil. But the actual content of peace—more elusive at any time than that of war—was scarcely grasped. Indeed, for a long time peace was understood in a negative fashion, simply as the absence of war. Later, from the end of the fifth century BC in Greece, and from the end of the Republic in Rome, when the picture became more sombre, peace was assigned an increasingly positive value. It was then that Praxiteles' father, Cephisodotus, carved its image; that it appeared on the bas-reliefs of the Altar of the Peace of Augustus (the *Ara Pacis Augusti*), and that its cult spread. Significantly, it acquired this positive valuation only in a-political terms, under the influence of the new philosophies (Cynic, Stoic, and Epicurean) which identified the happiness of the individual with the search for tranquillity, implying a rejection of civic values and a quest for inner peace within the human soul. Peace achieved value by being abstracted from war rather than by being positively defined as the opposite of war.

It is paradoxical that the ancients were so unsuccessful at 'thinking through' war, when it absorbed so much of their time and energy. Perhaps this was because it was so widespread and perennial that it appeared to be outside human initiative and to fall within the domain of nature or the realm of the gods. Thus it could be conceived as a principle of cosmic organisation, but not analysed as a regulative law of human society. The same could be said, incidentally, of the phenomenon of slavery, which in the theoretical thinking of the ancients occupies a minimal place far out of line with its importance in reality, for reasons that are not purely hypocritical.

In contrast, forced to take cognisance of the effectiveness of human interventions in constitutional development and constitutional struggles, the ancients discovered political philosophy. It was only in this context that the existence of real choices raised concretely and insistently the question of ends. The conceptual status of war was therefore subordinated to political thought. Even when it was considered on its own, war was treated as a means to some political end. Being simply a means, it could be the subject only of an essentially technical assessment. This is why, in ancient literature, political writing and military writing belong to two parallel 'cultures' following different lines of development.

The Ancient Strategists

Most of the ancients took Homer to be the founder of tactical theory, as he was of many other branches of knowledge. However, tactics gave rise to works of a technical nature only from the first half of the fourth century BC, under the influence of the Sophists, when war began to make demands which often ran contrary to the political development of the Greek city-states. It was then that Aeneas the Tactician, apparently a mercenary leader with a good enough education and a solid measure of common sense, published a kind of military encyclopedia of which only one book, on the defence of fortified positions, has come down to us. To the end of antiquity there were many emulators of Aeneas, including men as famous as Pyrrhus, king of Epirus, his son Alexander, and his adviser, the Thessalian Cineas, the historian Polybius and the Stoic philosopher Posidonius of Apamea.

Throughout the Byzantine period these works on military technique retained a practical interest and value as models. They gave rise to countless summaries, interpolations and adaptations, mostly without any originality. Their doctrines were even repeated by writers who were trying to provide more precisely for the needs of their own time. In the West the tradition was less vigorous during the Middle Ages, though Vegetius was translated into French by Jean de Meung, and into Italian by Bono Gimaboni. It then revived with the advent of the Renaissance: both directly, in the form of translations, paraphrases and abridgements, and also indirectly but no less clearly in the works of those engaged in advancing the art of war. For nearly three centuries, in fact, the battle between the ancients and the moderns was fought on this front too (and this ought to discourage us from exaggerating the qualitative change which was introduced, at least in men's consciences if not in practice, by the invention of firearms). In 1727, the Chevalier de Folard, the most prolific and esteemed theorist of his time, still felt no hesitation in proclaiming the superiority of the catapult over the cannon in siege warfare, and even at the end of that century the great Carnot, 'the organiser of victory', was still going so far, in his treatise on fortifications, as to advise the use of slings and cross-bows to protect the crossing of the moat.

Towards a Modern History of Ancient War

So long as military history remained a battlefield for professionals who were defending their careers at the same time as their ideas, it was impossible to study warfare other than in a narrowly utilitarian and pragmatic spirit, hardly compatible with the impartiality of the true critical mind (when, indeed, the study was not being used for purposes of edification). With continued technical progress such controversies lost their justification, but for a long time they continued to influence the professional standing of those who studied the subject, and the orientation of their work. A historian of ancient armies was still expected to be an experienced and well-tried practitioner. The Chevalier de Folard held it against certain of his predecessors, such as Justus Lipsius or Father Daniel, that they had not grown old in the saddle. The specialists in Kriegskunst who proliferated in the German Empire at the end of the nineteenth century and the beginning of the twentieth, made the most of their military record, or if they were in the position of having to apologise for their civilian status, their prefaces would refer at length to their sponsorship by the cream of the general staff.

Virtually all the manuals we possess date from this period, dominated by a generally positivist climate of opinion. Hence the principal object of almost all of them is to establish 'facts', more or less by analogy with modern techniques. There is certainly much to be learnt from this 'actual' analysis, but such a conception cannot fail to appear very limited and limiting to us today. In effect, it confines itself to the technical problems of armament, organisation and tactics which, when treated on their own, appear to possess within themselves the principles by which they develop. It tends to reduce the history of war to that of military operations, to the battle-stories which, like set-pieces, are mechanically inserted into the histories of ancient societies.

To these late nineteenth-century specialists who had experienced the limited confrontations of their own day and who remembered the 'piecemeal' wars of the last century, war was insubstantial and unreal, as gratuitous as a game of chance, an outlet for the energies of a social group which it did not affect deeply, or else a luxury activity. Hence the temptation to imagine war in antiquity, similarly, as a sort of *deus ex machina*, an inexhaustible source of accidents, which intervened from without to alter frontiers and to make and break empires. Sometimes it simply touched upon, and sometimes it radically upset, the course of history; history itself being reduced to that of the states. This conception is still the favourite weapon of those who are anxious to reduce ancient history to a fortuitous aggregation of heterogeneous civilisations 'miraculous' in origin and subject to mutations of a catastrophic nature.

In so far as historical research is now carried out at a much deeper level, liberated from the grip of positivist and 'humanist' tendencies and opened to the influence of other human sciences, the total character of contemporary wars, whether foreign or civic, has helped us to discern that ancient war has a reality, a manner of being, a practice and a mode of behaviour that are as wide as society itself. We have rediscovered the function of war on the community level, with its institutions, its rites, its ideology representing the reactions aroused in any given society by the natural, if not permanent threat of the foreigner. We can now also understand the ancient *homo militaris*, at the individual level with his ways of behaviour, ambitions and personal values, even though these are inextricably linked to those of the 'political', 'economic' and 'religious' man with whom he identifies himself. Since experience has taught us that war can no longer be considered as a pathological phenomenon alien to the normal course of events, we can no longer justify treating the military history of the Greeks and Romans as an isolated chapter of ancient history for the satisfaction of the intellectual foibles of some retired colonel.

1

The Legal Aspects of Ancient War

WAR AND THE STATE

War is both a law of nature and a human invention, a reality that is experienced and at the same time a legal construct. The ancient concept of war, as we find it established by the beginning of the classical period, the high point of the Greek city-state, did not embrace all social violence. It implied a confrontation between two distinct political communities demanding total commitment from their members. It further assumed that the communities engaged were willing, and able, to impose upon their fighting men the obligation to respect a certain code of war, which was, as we shall see, as binding in principle as it was vague in its practical applications.

Such a conception of war was profoundly influenced by the development of the idea of the State, that is, by the establishment of a truly political framework within which social solidarity was effective in a more or less authoritarian way. This conception belongs to the world of the cities and to a lesser extent of kingdoms, a world which gradually became established in limited and particularly favourable areas of the Mediterranean basin during the first half of the first millennium BC, and which later imposed its hegemony on neighbouring barbarian peoples, among whom it acquired the value of a model.

Clearly, no legal and ideological reconstruction elaborated in this way upon historically determined political bases can take account of the phenomenon of war in antiquity in its entirety, not even if we exclude, as the ancients themselves often did, the internal manifestations within any given community. By definition, so to speak, it excludes all hostile relations before the formation of states.

Warfare in the Homeric World

If we retrace our steps through time it is possible to get back

23

to a pre-judicial phase of war by analysing the oldest literary documents, and by reflecting upon the difficulties the classical authors encountered in understanding and describing the military events of their past.

Homer's account of the great expedition launched by the Atreides against Troy for the purpose of avenging the rape of Helen has, in effect, preserved a memory of the conflicts which were the normal fate of heroes. Usually they were very limited operations both as to objectives and as to the number of men involved. They did not mobilise the entire human and material resources of a people. They were conducted, so to speak, on a private basis by one of the kings or princes who formed the backbone of Homeric society, supported by a fluctuating mass of companions and servants who were united with them, more or less temporarily, by bonds of personal dependence or by a common objective. The chieftain was not necessarily obliged to obtain the endorsement of his collective group, and in this sense his action was a-political, for it did not directly concern the *demos*, the 'people'. Similarly his action was not aimed at imposing upon his adversaries a new legal situation affecting them as a community. It took the form of a raid across territorial boundaries or of piracy on the high seas, and it came to an end once the booty was captured.

Such an antagonism between groups acting often on their own initiative, with no mandate from their communities, in no way implies a true state of war between the communities: it can co-exist with unbroken relations on other levels, which, in turn, do not imply the regularity and stability of a true state of peace. Thus, everything occurs as if there were a tacit agreement to restrict hostilities within certain bounds. If travellers in the past are to be believed, many African, American and Oceanic tribes once lived in this state of micro-war or pseudo-peace, traditionally stealing each others' and capturing each others' women, without ever converting such behaviour into a reason for total war.

War and Peace in Early Rome

The history of early Rome is filled with similar episodes, which were difficult for the classical Roman historians to understand and interpret on the basis of purely annalistic information.

Livy in particular makes no attempt to conceal his difficulties: 'For the next three years' (493–490 BC), 'there was neither settled peace nor open war" (II, 21, 1).

'With the Volsci during the Latin War there was neither war nor peace" (II, 22, 1).

In 489

> a fresh alarm was created at Rome by the Sabines, but it was more a sudden raid than a regular war (II, 26, 1). From that time (475) there was neither peace nor war with the Veientes, and the affair became rather like brigandage. The Veientes retired into their city before the Roman legions; then, when they found that the latter were withdrawn, they made inroads into the countryside, evading war by keeping quiet, and then making quiet impossible by war (II, 48, 5–6). The Gauls, an unknown people, had recently overrun that part of Etruria, and they were neither on terms of assured peace with them, nor in open war (V, 17, 8).

These examples, easily multiplied, cast doubt not so much on the information of the historian writing in the age of Augustus, as upon the possibility—given his inadequate concepts and anachronistic vocabulary—of his characterising, let alone of his understanding, what really happened so long before.

This sporadic warfare, this incomplete peace, was not confined to the adversaries of Rome. Although Livy was inclined to credit the founders of the Roman city with the same notion of the State which his own contemporaries displayed, yet in the first books of his *History* he sometimes allows us to glimpse Roman military undertakings of a different type—'conspiracies' based upon a social solidarity of the pre-state type. An example of this is the war waged by the Fabian *gens*, in 475, against the Etruscan town of Veii.

> The Veientes, [Livy writes (II, 48, 7–49, 4)] a persistent rather than a formidable foe, created more irritation than alarm because it was never safe to neglect them or to turn attention elsewhere. Under these circumstances the Fabii came to the Senate; there the consul, on behalf of his house, spoke as follows: 'As you are aware, senators, the Veientine war does not require a large force so much as

one constantly in the field. Let the other wars be your care, leave the Fabii to deal with the Veientes. We will guarantee that the majesty of Rome shall be safe in that quarter. We propose to carry on that war as a private war of our own at our own cost. Let the State be spared money and men there.

A very hearty vote of thanks was passed. . . . News of what had happened spread through the whole city, the Fabii were praised to the skies; people said, 'One family has taken up the burden of the State, the Veientine war has become a private concern, a private quarrel. If there were two houses of the same strength in the City, and the one claimed the Volsci for themselves, the other the Aequi, then all the neighbouring states could be subjugated while Rome itself remained in profound tranquillity.' The next day the Fabii took their arms and assembled at the appointed place. The consul, wearing his commander's cloak, went out into the vestibule and saw the whole of his house drawn up in order of march. Taking his place in the centre, he gave the word of advance. Never has an army marched through the city smaller in numbers or with a more brilliant reputation or more universally admired. Three hundred and six soldiers, all patricians, all members of one house, not a single man of whom the senate, even in its palmiest days, would deem unfitted for high command, went forth, threatening ruin to the Veientes through the strength of a single family.

The Ritual Wars

The sources which throw light upon the gestation period of the ancient states, together with a comparative study of so-called primitive societies, make it possible to distinguish in the distant past of Greece more clearly than in that of Italy, another type of war, ritual in nature. Its ideal pattern, never fully realised, is as follows: between communities linked to each other by traditional ties of neighbourhood and of kinship, wars, rather like long-term tournaments or competitions (*agones*), take place periodically within a religious context of a mythical or cultural nature, according to rules which restrict the object and the extent of the conflict.

The best example is provided by the Argives and the Spartans, constantly at loggerheads over the possession of Thyreae, a poor mountain area on their common frontier. This rivalry went back to the legendary origins of Sparta, and it gave rise, according to the chronographers, to memorable wars from the eighth century B C onwards.

The first of these which is well known to us took place about the middle of the sixth century in the following conditions, according to Herodotus (I, 82):

> The Argives . . . agreed in conference with the Spartans that three hundred picked men a side should fight it out, and that Thyreae should belong to the victors; the rest of the two armies were to go home without staying to watch the fight, lest either side, seeing its champions getting the worst of it, might be tempted to intervene. On these terms they parted, leaving behind the men chosen to represent them, and the battle began. So closely was it contested that of the six hundred men only three were left alive—two Argives, Alcenor and Chromios, and one Spartan, Othryadas—and even these would have been killed had not darkness put an end to the fighting. The two Argives claimed the victory and hurried back to Argos; but the Spartan, Othryadas remained under arms and, having stripped the bodies of the Argive dead, carried their equipment to his own camp.
>
> The two armies met again on the following day, to learn the result of the battle. For a while both Argives and Spartans maintained that they had won, the former because they had the greater number of survivors, the latter because the two Argives had run away, whereas their own man had remained on the battlefield and stripped the bodies of the dead. The argument ended in blows, and a fresh battle began, in which after severe losses on both sides the Spartans were victorious. From that day the Argives, who previously by custom wore their hair long, began to clip it close and passed a law calling down imprecations on any man who let his hair grow, and on any woman who wore gold until Thyreae was recovered. The Spartans also adopted a new custom, but in precisely the opposite sense:

they used not to grow their hair long, but from that time they began to do so. It is said that Othryadas, the sole survivor of the three hundred, was ashamed to return to Sparta after the death of his companions and killed himself at Thyreae.

During the following century these battles continued to occur periodically as is shown by a passage from Thucydides (V, 41, 2–3) concerning the conclusion of a treaty of alliance between Argos and Sparta in 420:

What the Argives first demanded was that they might be allowed to refer to the arbitration of some state or private person the question of the Cynurian land, a piece of frontier territory about which they have always been disputing, and which contains the towns of Thyreae and Anthene and is occupied by the Spartans. The Spartans first said they could not allow this point to be discussed but that they were ready to conclude upon the old terms. Eventually, however, the Argive ambassadors succeeded in obtaining from them this concession: For the present there was to be a truce for fifty years, but it should be competent for either party, there being neither plague nor war in Sparta or Argos, to give formal challenge and decide the question of this territory by battle, as on a former occasion when both sides claimed victory; pursuit not being allowed beyond the frontier of Argos or Sparta. The Spartans at first thought this mere folly but at last, anxious at any cost to have the friendship of Argos, they agreed to the terms demanded, and put them in writing.

This peace was to be broken three years later, but the periodic battles continued right up to the Hellenistic period, after Philip II of Macedon had attempted to make both parties respect the original boundaries, and indeed even later, since towards the middle of the second century AD the Romans were again obliged to send to Greece a senator charged with 'making a settlement between the Lacedaemonians and the Argives on the subject of the disputed territory'. (Pausanias VII, 11, 1.)

There was another long-term war, equally famous, between the Euboean cities of Chalcis and Eretria over possession of the small Lelantine plain. In mythical times this plain had been the object of a battle between the Abantes (that is, the Euboeans) and the Kouretes who on this occasion cut their hair short so that the enemy would not be able to grasp it and who, after their defeat emigrated to Aetolia. Later, between the eighth and sixth centuries, the Eretrians and Chalcidians suspended their friendly collaboration from time to time for a little honest fighting over the frontier areas.

> In general [according to Strabo (X, 1, 12)] these cities were in accord with one another, and when differences arose concerning the Lelantine plain they did not so completely break off relations as to wage their wars in all respects according to the will of each, but they came to an agreement as to the conditions under which they were to conduct the fight. This is shown by a certain inscribed pillar which forbids the use of long-range missiles.*

The same characteristics are to be found in several other long-term wars: those between the Thessalians and the Phocaeans, between the Erythraeans and the Chians, between the Samians and the Prienians, and finally between the Athenians and the Boeotians over the regions of Oropos, Oinoe, Panactos and Melainai. But well into the Hellenistic period the most fruitful field for study in this respect is Crete, a treasure house of Greek traditions. Its history is one long succession of local conflicts over small frontier territories containing sanctuaries, ending regularly with the conclusion of treaties of peace and alliance which were as detailed as they were precarious.

For most modern historians, this type of war can be satisfactorily explained only by reference to the rites of initiation which, at the dawn of ancient societies, brought about and consecrated the integration of adolescents into the adult warrior community.

Now the practice of initiation rites presupposes the division of the young into age-classes subject, over the years, to certain religious and educational obligations. After this training, which lasted for varying lengths of time and came to an end soon after puberty, there were public ceremonies, similar to those

* This stele was deposited at Amarynthus in the sanctuary to Artemis, whose cult included military parades and competitions of armed dancers.

encountered in most 'rites of passage'. These consisted, first of separation rites, which detached the candidate from the inferior community of women and children; then there followed a period of segregation on the outskirts of the community, often on its territorial frontiers in places subject to the wild forces of nature and haunted by supernatural powers; that it is to say, in a universe which was antithetical to the social universe. Then finally came the rites of admission, characterised by probationary tests which revealed the new skills of the adolescent who, after undergoing a fictitious and simulated death, was reborn into the bosom of the superior community of adults.

Of course, this pattern of initiation, in so far as we have been able to derive it from a comparative study of primitive societies, was already disappearing in Greece in the historical period: the surviving residue varied in forms and in ways of adaptation to the social and political development which led to the formation of the ancient states. The recourse to collective and egalitarian techniques of integration became more and more restricted by the increasing heterogeneity of the social body. The need for the ancient techniques was removed by the establishment of bonds of religious dependence and of genuinely political power; these were now the factors which ensured, from the outside, so to speak, the internal stability and cohesion of the group.

So it was that the initiation tests were altered in order to correspond more closely to the new needs of community life. In some instances they assumed an essentially educational character. The practices associated with the period of segregation gave rise to the institution of the *ephebeia*, while the individual trials of strength turned into ritual wars between neighbouring peoples or between different age-classes. Or they took on a non-military competitive ('agonistic') character, through a crystallisation of the religious factor into an autonomous one: this is shown particularly by the foundation of the Olympic Games, the most ancient and most prestigious manifestation of the Greek agonistic spirit. The quadrennial rhythm of the celebration, the division of the competitors into age-classes, the way of life prescribed for them before the contests, the partial exclusion of women, the presence of the 'whip-master' to ensure order—they are all reminders of the older initiation ceremonies practised in this frontier area by the young men of Piso and Elis before these games were thrown open to all the Greeks in 776 BC. In Sparta, similarly, we can follow from the classical to the Roman period the progressive transformation of an initiation combat between age-classes into an ordeal in the agonistic spirit: in the time of Pausanias (III, 16, 9–11), rival bands of young Spartiates no longer fought each other in ritual battles around the altar of Artemis Orthis, but competed there in tests of endurance under the whip, risking their lives to win the title of 'victor at the altar' (*bomonikes*).

The ritual wars were, therefore, essentially, wars 'for internal use only', aimed far more at increasing the intrinsic value of the community than at warding off some pressing danger. Their function was one of regulating society rather than defending it, to meet the needs of the social structure, felt 'spontaneously' by the community even when there were no external pressures. It is then easy to understand that their *raison d'être*, just like that of other initiation rites, was bound to dwindle as the society evolved and the concept of the State became established. For now the community was organised and preserved more effectively and more regularly on the material, institutional and ideological levels, without resort to military mimes and incantations designed to arouse the spirit of discipline and of solidarity indispensable for the survival of the community.

Piracy and Brigandage

The age-class, with its initiation practices, was not the only elementary solidarity group conceivable in a society of a pre-state type. There were others, depending chiefly on kinship or its substitutes (for example the clientship), or at a later stage upon territory, which in a natural way permanently ensured the minimum of social cohesion not at first guaranteed in unstable communities often based on brute force. 'Private' wars were, then, characteristic of an archaic world in which 'politics' were not yet the effective reality and often withdrew before natural principles of organisation. (Such wars were presumably subject to a certain ritual less familiar than that which surrounds the rites we have already studied.) At this stage of historical evolution such wars did not rupture the social contract; this is suggested by the adjective 'private'. They simply demonstrated the unfinished and precarious nature of the contract and the

31

preponderance of pre-political structures in the life of the community.

The elementary forms of solidarity were bound to become atrophied or profoundly altered when the political forms were imposed upon them. What, for example, would have become of them in the city of Plato's *Laws* (XII, 955 B–C), which required total commitment from the citizen in military matters?

> Everyone shall regard the friend or enemy of the state as his own personal friend or enemy; and if anyone makes peace or war with any parties privately and without public consent, in his case also the punishment shall be death; and if any section of the state makes peace or war on its own account with any parties, the generals shall summon the author of this action before the court, and the penalty for him who is convicted shall be death.

The creation of cities and the constitution of kingdoms reduced the frequency of 'private' wars though of course piracy and brigandage continued where central authority was too weak to prevent them.

In societies accustomed to 'private' wars, piracy carried no particular stigma. Among the Greeks of the olden days, Thucydides reports (I, 5):

> No disgrace was yet attached to such an achievement, but even some glory. An illustration of this is furnished by the honour with which some of the inhabitants of the continent still regard a successful marauder, and by the question we find the old poets everywhere representing the people as asking of travellers—'Are they pirates?'—as if those who are asked the question would have no idea of disclaiming the imputation, or their interrogators of reproaching them for it.

In Homer's time, to which the historian is referring, and even during the later archaic period, it was especially difficult to distinguish between merchants and pirates. Both professions were practised by the Taphians and the Phoenicians in the *Odyssey,* and also by the Phocaeans who roamed the western Mediterranean in the sixth century in their fifty-oared warships. These sea-rovers were fortunate in possessing the favour of Hermes ever since the time of Autolycus, the Homeric hero 'who excelled all men in thievery and in oaths' (*Odyssey*, XIX, 395). Even Solon who started Athens on the road that led to democracy admitted that piracy was within the law.

Ever since, certain Mediterranean peoples made a speciality of this way of life, either because they inhabited land of poor quality, or because they appreciated more than others the advantages of a predatory economy. All along the rocky or marshy coasts, among all the islands and inlets—which is tantamount to saying the whole length of the Mediterranean coast, wherever little fleets of light craft could benefit from the element of surprise and then fall back in safety to their hideouts, and especially near the great commercial routes, piracy was endemic. From Cilicia to Caria, in the Black Sea, in the islands of the Aegean and particularly around Crete, from Aetolia to the valley of the Po, from the mouth of the Tiber to the delta of the Rhone, in Corsica, in Sardinia and in the Lipari Islands, not to mention the African coast, men held themselves ready to raid, more or less as if that were their craft.

In order to contain such natural inclinations, a power had to be capable of policing the seas to its own benefit, and, indirectly, to everybody else's. According to tradition, that was the way that Minos and Theseus established their reputations as civilising heroes. This responsibility was later assumed by the Athenians in the eastern Mediterranean, especially during the period of the confederacy of Delos, then by Alexander of Macedon and the Ptolemaic rulers, finally by the Rhodians up till the middle of the second century BC. Then the duty fell to the Romans, who had been exercising it more or less effectively in the western Mediterranean ever since the middle of the fourth century, but not in the Mediterranean basin as a whole until the Empire.

As efforts at pacification were pursued, with varying success, so the status of piracy altered. There was no longer a place for it in the network of peaceful or warlike obligations which the organised states were striving to establish with each other. Little by little piracy was losing the autonomous field of action it had hitherto enjoyed thanks to the inadequacy of the state structures; it was slipping into illegality, since it satisfied neither conditions of peace nor those of war. That is why the moral discredit and the sanctions affecting pirates became increasingly severe; they were now guilty not only of ignoring but also of defying the common laws of humanity.

More or less excluded from the social body, piracy then took refuge, so to speak, on the geographic frontiers of Greco-Roman legality. It did not however set itself up as an independent power, but simply infiltrated itself into the already existing political framework of certain barbarian or semi-barbarian groups. Thereafter the struggle against piracy entailed the destruction of actual pirate-states, accomplished by the Romans.

Their first adversaries were the Tyrrhenians who, based along the Tuscan coast and supported by other Italic peoples, ravaged the seas from the Aegean to the Straits of Gibraltar until the whole of Etruria fell to the Romans at the beginning of the third century BC.*

The next preoccupation of the Romans was Illyria. During the reigns of Agron and Teuta its sea-raiding increased to the point where it exercised a sort of hegemony over the Straits of Otranto. Queen Teuta, apparently less successful than her predecessor in imposing her authority upon a strong tribal aristocracy, was forced, on assuming the throne, to 'grant letters of marque to privateers authorising them to plunder all they fell in with'. (Polybius II, 4, 8). The Romans, motivated by strategic rather than by commercial interests, intervened for the first time in 229–228, with the support of Demetrius of Pharos, and deprived Teuta of access to the southern Adriatic, and a second time, in 219, in order to break the power of Demetrius who had himself taken over Teuta's practices and had moreover struck up an alliance with Philip V of Macedon. Illyria now came under a sort of Roman protectorate, but in the rein of Genthius new difficulties arose; piracy flared up again, and continued until the Illyrian king was defeated in 168, during the third Macedonian War. Thereafter the peace of this region was no longer disturbed. However, the same cannot be said for the rest of the Adriatic. Rome was forced to intervene there on several occasions, in 158, in 129, and in 119 against the Iapyges and

* In the western Mediterranean the last strongholds of the pirates were not, however, to disappear until the middle of the second century B.C., after the occupation of Liguria and the submission of Carthage.

the Dalmatians whose pillaging instincts were again aroused in the first century, favoured by the civil wars which were then ravaging the heart of the Roman Empire.

The Aetolians, who had long enjoyed a well-established reputation for piracy in Greece, did not alter their methods even when, at the beginning of the Hellenistic period, they found themselves at the head of an important confederation. Their military code remained peculiar to themselves; alone of all the Greeks, they assumed the right to 'take spoil from spoil' according to an expression whose meaning Philip V of Macedon explained to Flamininus:

> When Flamininus expressed some wonder at what he meant by this, the king tried to explain it to him by saying that 'the Aetolian custom was this. They not only plundered those with whom they were at war, and harried their country; but, if certain other nations were at war with each other, even though both were friends and allies of the Aetolians, none the less the Aetolians might, without a formal decree of the people, take part with both combatants and plunder the territory of both. The result was that in the eyes of the Aetolians there were no defined limits of friendship or enmity, but they were ready to be enemies and assailers of all who had a dispute on anything'. (Polybius XVIII, 4, 8–5, 3).

However the Roman attitude to the Aetolians was not dictated by such considerations. The deciding factor, in this case too, was the important role the Aetolians were playing in Greece, either in alliance with Macedonia and the Achaean League, or in opposition to them. Their promise to Antiochus III that the whole of Greece 'would muster on the shores as soon as his fleet was sighted' sealed their fate at the hands of the Romans in 189. Piracy disappeared forthwith from this region of Greece.

Trachinian Cilicia in Asia Minor had retained a certain independence within the Ptolemaic and Seleucid Empires, thanks to its mountainous terrain, its inhospitable shores and the aggressive temperament of its inhabitants. So it gradually became a rallying point for pirates, especially after Diodotus Tryphon appealed to them, around 140, to support his struggle against the commercial towns of the Syrian coast. From their fortresses in Coracesium, these sea-rovers succeeded in imposing their authority upon the local dynasties of the whole of Cilicia, Isauria, Pamphylia and Eastern Lycia, without arousing any response from the Romans who were initially only too pleased with the way the pirates were providing slaves for the Delos market. However, in 102 the Romans took action—not, it is true, very effectively—and they then passed a law which invited the neighbouring Hellenistic rulers to take their own measures against piracy. Rome in fact did not feel itself directly threatened by the expansion of Cilician piracy until the pirates placed themselves entirely at the service of Mithridates VI Eupator. The pirates, organised into powerful squadrons, guaranteed the control of the seas to that king for many years, launching punitive operations against Roman installations in the east whenever they could. Once the Cilician pirates were politically committed in this way, the energies of the Romans were once more aroused. Pompey, who was entrusted with extensive powers by the *lex Gabinia* put an end to their activity in 67 BC.

Brigandage within the Roman Empire, for its part, became more widespread from the middle of the second century AD, with the growing crisis in the central power. The most suitable terrain was provided by the barely Romanised mountainous regions and by the inhospitable fringes along the frontiers, where discontent could assume quite a developed political character when national traditions were revived or through collaboration with barbarian invaders. From the third century onwards the operations of the Bacaudae in Gaul, and of the Circumcellions in Africa for instance took on alarming proportions and even constituted a direct threat to the unity of the Empire.

Ancient piracy and brigandage are fundamentally ambiguous phenomena. Fed by individual rebellion, by social unease, by resistance to either Hellenisation or Romanisation, they tended sometimes to anarchy, sometimes to an approximation of either civil war or foreign war. The only characteristic in common was their rejection of established institutions and values which they attacked from within at their point of least resistance and in their moments of crisis. In this respect they were diametrically opposed to organised societies as these were conceived, for example, by Cicero in the *Republic* (I, 25) :

> *Scipio*: The commonwealth, then, is the people's affair; and the people is not every group of men, associated in any manner, but is the coming together of a considerable number of men who are united by a common agreement about law and rights and by the desire to participate in mutual advantages.

So it is that piracy and brigandage reveal the reverse of Greco–Roman legality, and enable us to glimpse its limits, its failures and imperfections. Considered by Aristotle (*Politics,* 1256a36) to be a natural method of acquisition, they were, so to speak, 'anti-wars' lacking the validation of law and ultimate victory. By a simple reversal of perspective, they can be equated with the notion of the state itself, as by St Augustine: (*City of God,* IV, 4–6):

> And so if justice is left out, what are kingdoms except great robber bands? For what are robber bands except little kingdoms? The band also is a group of men governed by the orders of a leader, bound by a social compact, and its booty is divided according to a law agreed upon. If by repeatedly adding desperate men this plague grows to the point where it holds territory and establishes a fixed seat, seizes cities and subdues peoples, then it more conspicuously assumes the name of kingdom, and this name is now openly granted to it, not for any subtraction of cupidity, but by addition of impunity . . . Now to make war on one's neighbours and from them to move on against the rest, crushing and subduing peoples who have given no offence, out of mere lust for dominion—what else can this be called except brigandage on a grand scale?

The Right of Reprisal

Reprisal operations, which continued until a late date in certain sectors of the ancient world were equally close in principle to 'private' wars.

The right of reprisal is founded upon widespread primitive

custom, which entails a certain solidarity, for better or for worse, among the members of a community: if one of them injures the person or the belongings of a stranger, the latter has the right to insist upon reparation in any place or at any time, not only from the guilty party but also from the other members of the group, who must themselves seek compensation from the offender. Private conflicts of this kind could easily culminate in a genuine state of war between the communities involved, kinship groups and later, cities. Hence the necessity, fully appreciated by both the Greeks and the Romans, of curtailing the development by laying down legal conditions for reprisals, when they found it impossible to settle the differences peacefully by judicial means.

Under these circumstances it appears that the taking of hostages was still allowed in seventh century Athens by one of Draco's laws, as quoted by Demosthenes (XXIII, 82):

> If any man die of a violent death, his kinsmen may take and hold hostages in respect of such death, until they either submit to trial for bloodguiltiness or surrender the actual manslayers. The right is limited to three hostages and no more.

The seizure of a stranger's goods had already in the time of Homer been more or less under the control of political authorities, as is proved by Nestor's account, in the *Iliad* (XI, 670–695) of his punitive expedition among the Eleans. Later on the state, when unable to suppress these ancestral customs, discovered it to be in its own interest to take matters even more firmly in hand, to the point of setting itself up as an entrepreneur, as happened among the Chalcedonians, in order to pay their mercenaries:

> . . . they made proclamation that anyone, either citizen or alien, who had right of reprisal against any city or individual, and wished to exercise it, should have his name entered on a list. A large number of names was enrolled and the people thus obtained a specious pretext for exercising reprisal upon ships that were passing on their way to the Black Sea. They accordingly arrested the ships and fixed a period within which they would consider any claims

that might be made in respect of them. Having now a large fund in hand, they paid off the mercenaries, and set up a tribunal to decide the claims; and those whose goods had been unjustly seized were compensated out of the revenues of the State. (Pseudo-Aristotle, *Oeconomica* II, 2, 10.)

To the extent that the public authorities intervened in the exercise of this right, they attempted to impose limits upon it, in theory at least. They either granted foreigners the right of 'asylum' which, as the Greek word shows, was originally intended to prevent this type of operation; or else, conversely, they intervened with foreign powers to ensure the immunity of their own people, either through diplomatic channels or by direct agreements with creditors. According to Isocrates (III, 33), Nicocles, king of Cyprus, proceeded in the latter manner:

And although Greece was closed to us because of the war which had arisen, and though we were being robbed on every side, I solved most of these difficulties, paying to some their claims in full, to others in part, asking some to postpone theirs, and satisfying others as to their complaints by whatever means I could.

Similarly, a fourth-century inscription from Cyrene reports that ambassadors went to several Greek cities, most of them in the Peloponnese, and paid the debts that individual Cyreneans had contracted, thereby annulling the reprisal rights exercised against all members of the community.*

In Italy, too, different forms of reprisal and private vengeance presumably once characterised relations among family groups, tribes and finally cities. However, from the time when Rome imposed her authority, towards the end of the fourth century BC, the state took charge. The Romans entrusted the resolution of such conflicts to a tribunal of *recuperatores,* chosen by the Senate from among its own members. Then, as the number of litigations continued to increase, the organisation for these tribunals was handed over, in 242, to a *peregrine*

* See Y. Garlan, in *Bulletin de Correspondence Hellénique* 89 (1965) pp. 338–39.

praetor (a magistrate in charge of the legal affairs of aliens); only major disputes which directly affected the Roman state continued to be the responsibility of the Senate. With further Roman expansion, the Senate soon found itself overwhelmed once more, this time by complaints against the abuses by magistrates in the conquered territories. To protect the provincials a permanent tribunal was created in 149, composed of jurors drawn from the Senate and empowered to receive complaints from citizens and non-citizens alike.

The Rights of Salvage

In principle the rights of salvage, like the right of reprisal, lay beyond the range of legal definitions of the state of war or the state of peace. This right was for a long time applied with extreme rigour to the profit of the inhabitants of the coastal regions or of their rulers who soon learnt how to operate as shipwreckers to their own advantage. When a stranger's ship foundered or he was forced to land outside the ports open to him, he could expect his cargo to be seized and himself to be enslaved, if he was not sacrificed to the native gods, as in the legend of Iphigenia in Taurus, or massacred as were Odysseus' companions by the Laestrygonians.

As the public authorities became strong enough to control maritime affairs, and as piracy diminished, so the right of salvage was restricted by certain rules, first applied, it appears, by the Phoenicians. In Greece the right was already disappearing in the classical period, although it was never completely eliminated on the barbarian frontiers of the Greco–Roman world. One such area was the coast of the Black Sea on either side of the Dardanelles, where in the third century B C treaties of immunity were still being drawn up (for example between the Thracian king, Sardalas, and the city of Mesembria, and between Ziaelas, king of Bithynia, and the island of Cos). In the western Mediterranean bilateral agreements to similar effect were concluded in the same period between the Etruscans, the Carthaginians and the Romans.

Efforts to curtail the right of salvage were more successful under the Roman Empire, as is proved by various strict stipulations in the *Digest*: but in the end, with the political and economic disorganisations which resulted from the barbaric invasions, the practice made its appearance again and continued to flourish during the Middle Ages.

In sum, as war became institutionalised under the aegis of organised states, its contours were marked out by opposing it to peace and by reducing the in-between, ambiguous zone of private hostilities, ritual wars and natural forms of pillage, alien in nature to formal, established law. The Greek cities thus came to agree more or less tacitly upon a number of international customs. Under the influence of Hellenistic philosophy and with the support of growing Roman power, this customary law tended in time to evolve into a doctrinal system.

THE DEFINITION OF THE STATE OF WAR

The ancients could not imagine a true war that was not limited in time by declarations, agreements, and symbolic acts. They often took a religious form, presumably so that the solemnity of the procedure should emphasise their official nature, but also because it was in the nature of things to associate the tutelary divinities with the violent changes brought about, in the organisation of the cosmos as well as in the life of states—by the opening and closing of hostilities. Given that the time of war and the time of peace were different in essence, no transition from one to the other could come about without due precaution and guarantees.

The Sacral Rhythm of War

The first characteristic of ancient war was therefore the way that it conformed to a 'sacral rhythm' particularly in the earliest epochs and especially in Rome. Because they wished to make war an activity which was both exterior to the city and yet integrated with it, the Romans took more pains than the Greeks to assign a defined domain to it, both temporally and spatially. They prohibited all military activity within the *pomerium*, the mystical precinct of the civil community, and they gave a religious definition to the season for war, even when this bore no relation to reality.

The seasonal rhythm of the consecration and deconsecration of military activity involved the following ceremonies. In the spring, during the months of February and March, the Salians started off by performing sacred dances to arouse the super-natural forces, striking their staves against the sacred shields (*ancilia*) one of which was said to have fallen from the heavens. Next, the military equipment was purified, in particular the horses, by holding races at the feast of the *Equirria*, and the trumpets on the day of the *tubilustrium*. In the autumn there was the purification of arms (*armilustrium*), and the 'October horse' was put to death (the horse on the right in the winning team in the chariot race on the Field of Mars).

Before leaving the city, the army underwent another lustra-tion rite, while its leader brandished the lance of Mars and shook the sacred Salian shields. Simultaneously, the doors of the temple of Janus were opened in accordance with a custom described by Virgil (*Aeneid*, VII, 1 601–15):

> There was a sacred custom in Latium, land of the west, which the Alban cities always observed, and Rome, supreme in all the world, observes today when Romans first stir Mars to engage battle, whether they prepare to launch war's miseries with might and main on Getae, Hyrcanians, or Arabs, or to journey to India, in the track of the dawn, and to bid the Parthians hand our standards back. There are twin Gates of War, for by that name men call them; and they are hallowed by men's awe and the dread presence of heartless Mars. A hundred bars of bronze, and iron's tough everlasting strength, close them, and Janus, never moving from that threshold, is their guard. When the Fathers of the City have irrevocably decided for battle, the consul himself, a figure conspicuous in Quirine toga of state and Gabine cincture, unbolts these gates, and their hinge-posts groan; it is he who calls the fighting forth, then the rest of their manhood follows, and the bronze horns, in hoarse assent, add their breath.

Was it war, or was it peace that was shut up in the temple? We do not know. What is certain is that the opening of its doors marked the opening of communications between Rome and its armies.

Similar precautions had to be observed throughout the dura-tion of a campaign. Both the Greeks and the Romans waited upon portents which manifested the will of the gods. If such

portents failed to appear they took the initiative by question-
ing the gods, either through sacrifices or by taking the auspices.
(The Roman general who held the *imperium* was entitled to
do this, with or without employing the augury and the sacred
fowl.) In times of danger the Romans even went so far as to
try to 'force the hand of the gods.' They either incited the enemy
gods to desert (*evocatio*), by swearing many promises to them,
or they made a sacrifice of substitution, supposed to bring them
victory in exchange for the life of their leader (*devotio*).

Lastly, these ceremonies of consecration were reinforced, as
we shall see, by religious guarantees which accompanied the
opening and closing of hostilities even though these had acquired
an essentially political character before the beginning of the
historical period.

The Right of Initiative

The right to decide upon the beginning and end of hostilities was the privilege of the organ of government which was
the depository of sovereign power. There were no exceptions to
this rule; it was always the last to succumb to any change in the
balance of power within the institutional framework of the
community.

In the early-state period, whatever the political regime (with
the partial exception of tyrannies), the initiative belonged to
the popular assemblies (whether or not they were open to all
citizens), usually after smaller councils had considered the
matter. Judging by Athens, the assemblies were required to make
a decision in this matter at regular intervals, regardless of circumstances: problems of defence were automatically on the
agenda of the principal assembly in each prytany, quite apart
from the special sessions summoned in times of crisis. In Rome,
whatever the role of the Senate in matters of diplomacy, the
final decision was the *iussus populi* expressed through the
comitia centuriata which represented the people in arms. These
comitia were still being summoned in the early Empire, to keep
up the appearance of legality, although the emperor was entitled to make sovereign decisions on these matters by virtue of
his military *imperium*. Even in certain Hellenistic monarchies
of a national type, such as the Macedonian, the people, represented by the army, were sometimes summoned in order to

ratify the royal decision by acclamation, and their participation was sometimes mentioned alongside the monarch in diplomatic agreements.

This real or ideal identification of the popular will with the right of initiative in foreign policy, which dated from the origins of community life, thus retained, under different guises, all its force as a principle of the institutional organisation of ancient states.

The Agents of Greek Diplomacy

In order to make practicable decisions in diplomatic matters and to put these into effect, it was necessary to be able to communicate with the foreign power in some way or other, whatever the current mutual feelings of the parties involved might be. Certain precautions were necessary, not only to ensure the safety of envoys, but also to limit their freedom of action lest this necessary delegation of power remove the least part of the authority of the sovereign body.

For these two reasons the earliest diplomatic relations in Greece were carried out by heralds, who were messengers entrusted with the exact transmission of an oral message from their sovereign. The Homeric heralds were recruited from among the servants (*therapontes*) surrounding the kings, in whose service they acquired both official and private functions (in so far as such a distinction can be made at this time). Their very title, *keryx* (related to Sanskrit *karuk*, meaning 'to sing'), the epithets describing them as 'quick', 'clear-voiced' and 'sonorous', the intellectual qualities of wisdom and good sense attributed to them, and also the revealing personal names they bore—all bear witness to the clarity and rapidity with which they had to acquit themselves of their duties.

However, ambassadors soon made their appearance alongside the heralds, whose duty it was to persuade and convince. Subtlety and prudence were the qualities that were demanded in the envoys. Odysseus was the perfect example, for from his lips words fell 'like snowflakes in winter'. In order to lend greater credibility to their proposals, on each occasion at least two were chosen from among the men of high standing, preferably from among those who were connected with the opposing side by bonds of friendship or kinship.

44

The condition and the role of heralds and ambassadors remained virtually unchanged in the classical period. The former were usually 'professionals' who either acted alone as 'letter-bearers' or were included in a delegation. In most cases it proved necessary to elect a commission of ambassadors (all with equal powers), who directly approached the other side's authorities, bringing written instructions and speaking in their support. As they were seldom invested with plenipotentiary powers, they might find themselves obliged to make several journeys to and fro before being in a position to conclude an agreement. Greek diplomatic procedures thus remained rudimentary and extremely rigid on account of both the sensitivity of the sovereign bodies and the amateurism of their representatives.

In the Hellenistic period the kings themselves sometimes took the negotiations in hand: the kings of Pergamum, for example, on occasion came in person to plead their cause before the Roman Senate. Usually however ambassadors continued to be used. They were men of high quality or of high rank, chosen as much for their prestige as for their ability—friends or relations of the king, *proxenoi*, higher magistrates, men of science, artists, philosophers or orators—and the rank of these representatives increased as the conclusion of the negotiations was neared. The decline in political life tended, moreover, to simplify the diplomatic game somewhat by introducing the idea of the delegation of power, and even, in exceptional circumstances, by recourse to more or less secret negotiations.

The Agents of Roman Diplomacy

At the beginning of Roman history as of that of many other Italic peoples, diplomacy was essentially the responsibility of a college of priests known as the *fetiales*, a word derived from the Indo–European root *dhe* ('to place'). They had the task of establishing the *fas*, the mystical base in the invisible world without which any enterprise commanded or authorised by *ius*, and in more general terms any human enterprise at all, was bound to be uncertain, calamitous, even fatal.

According to Dionysius of Halicarnassus (II, 72),

> They are chosen men from the best families and they exercise their holy office for life. King Numa was also the first

who instituted this holy magistracy among the Romans. But whether he took his example from those called the Aequicoli, according to the opinion of some, or from the city of Ardea, as Gellius writes, I cannot say. It is sufficient for me to state that before Numa's reign the college of *fetiales* did not exist among the Romans. It was instituted by Numa when he was on the point of making war on the people of Fidenae, who had raided and ravaged his territories, in order to see whether they would come to an accommodation with him without war; and that is what they actually did, being constrained by necessity. But since the college of the *fetiales* is not in use among the Greeks, I think it is incumbent upon me to relate how many and how great affairs fall under its jurisdiction to the end that those who are unacquainted with the piety practised by the Romans of those times may not be surprised to find that all their wars had the most successful outcome; for it will appear that the origins and motives of them all were most holy, and for this reason especially the gods were propitious to them in the dangers that attended them.

The multitude of duties, to be sure, that fall within the province of these *fetiales* makes it no easy matter to enumerate them all; but to indicate them by a summary outline, they are as follows: It is their duty to take care that the Romans do not enter upon an unjust war against any city in alliance with them, and if others begin the violation of treaties against them, to go as ambassadors and first make formal demand for justice, and then, if the others refuse to comply with their demands, to sanction war. In like manner, if any people in alliance with the Romans complain of having been injured by them and demand justice, these men are to determine whether they have suffered anything in violation of their alliance; and if they find their complaints well-grounded, they are to seize the accused and deliver them up to the injured parties. They are also to take cognizance of the crimes committed against ambassadors, to take care that treaties are religiously observed, to make peace, and if they find that peace has been made otherwise than is prescribed by the holy laws, to set it aside; and to enquire into and to expiate the transgressions of the generals in so far as they relate to oaths and treaties.

However, when war moved away from the boundaries of the Roman territory the role of the *fetiales* tended to dwindle, for then they served merely as a magico-legal cover for the initiative of the Senate and its representatives. From the middle of the third century BC negotiations with foreigners were conducted by legates, chosen generally by the Senate from within its own ranks, and usually ten in number. Thus the stipulations of the fetial law took on an increasingly symbolic character, and eventually fell into disuse. True, they were resuscitated from time to time; now and then in the early Empire on land near the Roman temple of Bellona, which by a fiction was assimilated to enemy territory, and, even more rarely, along the frontiers, until the end of the Late Empire. In reality, all power in diplomatic matters was wielded by the emperors and their personal envoys.

The Declaration of War

The primary function of all these diplomatic agents was to prepare for the opening of hostilities. Before the crucial moment which was to unleash forces of destruction of unpredictable character and dimensions, it was essential to have the right on one's side, in the eyes of the gods even more than in the eyes of men; formally at least, by a judicious selection of the *casus belli*, and above all by scrupulously respecting the traditional rites involved in the declaration of war.

The *casus belli* could only be one of legitimate defence. In the Platonic dialogue that bears his name Alcibiades states, 'even if someone decides that he must go to war with those who are doing what is just, he would not admit that they were doing so' (109c). In such a situation the best thing to do was to invoke the defence or interests of the gods, or the interests of the community, or even the interests of one's allies. Thus a large field of possibilities was open to anyone wishing to camouflage an act of aggression under honourable motives. The first category of complaints comprised not only obvious manifestations of impiety but also any violation of existing treaties or any infringement upon privileges of immunity, both of which were, as we shall see, placed under divine protection. The second type of grievance could be interpreted just as widely, but was invoked mainly in cases of actual attack upon territory. The purpose was usually to establish beyond question the division of responsibilities: allies, who were not normally required to support a war of aggression, were in this way compelled to take part in the campaign.

Once the *casus belli* was established, one would, unless it was a matter of urgency, make sure that the enemy refused to recognise or make amends for its wrongs, before proceeding to an official declaration of war and the symbolic religious acts which authorised the opening of a campaign. There were many Romans who went so far as to maintain that the opening rites sufficed for a *bellum pium et iustum*, without bothering about finding a 'just cause'. When an aggressor refused or failed to satisfy similar obligations, the Greeks for their part took the view that it was a 'war without proclamation by heralds' (*polemos akeryktos*) which meant, more or less, a war which could not be atoned for.

In Greece this process of laying the blame upon the other side appears to have been undertaken with a minimum of formality, essentially by word of mouth. It was obligatory to send heralds to 'announce the war', an action that might be confirmed by a number of ritual practices which were never strictly defined. One was to send a lamb across the frontier, symbolising the intention of the aggressors to ravage the country and turn it into pasture land. The Spartans, the most punctilious of all the Greeks on such matters of protocol, would take the precaution, when on the point of leaving their city and crossing their borders, of offering solemn sacrifices which enabled them to discover the disposition of the gods.

For the Romans, on the contrary, far removed from the Greek spirit of pragmatism, the declaration of war was an ideal occasion for deploying all the resources of their legalistic spirit. In the earliest years the college of *fetiales* performed a complicated ceremony which Livy describes in detail (I, 32, 5–14):

> Numa had instituted religious observance for times of peace; Ancus Marcius provided the ceremonies appropriate to a state of war. In order that wars might not be

only conducted but also proclaimed with some formality, he wrote down the law as taken from the ancient nation of the Aequieolae, under which the *fetiales* act down to this day when seeking redress for injuries.

The procedure is as follows: The ambassador binds his head in a woollen fillet. When he has reached the frontiers of the nation from whom satisfaction is demanded, he says, 'Hear, O Jupiter! Hear, ye confines', naming the particular nation whose they are, 'Hear, O Justice! I am the public herald of the Roman people. Rightly and duly authorised do I come; let confidence be placed in my words.' Then he recites the terms of the demands, and calls Jupiter to witness: 'If I am demanding the surrender of those men or those goods contrary to justice and religion, suffer me never more to enjoy my native land.' He repeats these words as he crosses the frontier, he repeats them to whoever happens to be the first person he meets, he repeats them as he enters the gates and again on entering the forum, with some slight changes in the wording of the formula. If his demand is refused at the expiration of thirty-three days (the fixed period of grace) he declares war in the following terms: 'Hear, O Jupiter, and thou, Janus Quirinus, and all ye heavenly gods, and ye gods of earth and of the lower world, hear me! I call you to witness that this people'—mentioning it by name—'is unjust and does not fulfil its sacred obligations. But about these matters we must consult the elders in our land in what way we may obtain our rights.'

With these words the ambassador returned to Rome for consultation. The king forthwith consulted the Senate in words to the following effect: 'Concerning the matters, suits and causes, whereof the Pater Patratus of the Roman people has complained to the Pater Patratus of the Ancient Latins and to the people of the Ancient Latins, which matters they were bound severally to surrender, discharge and make good, whereas they have done none of these things—say, what is your opinion?' He whose opinion was first asked replied, 'I am of opinion that they ought to be recovered by a just and righteous war, wherefore I give my consent and vote for it.' Then the others were asked in order, and when the majority of those present declared themselves of the same opinion, war was agreed upon.

It was customary for the *fetial* to carry to the enemy's frontiers a blood-smeared spear tipped with iron or burnt at the end, and, in the presence of at least three adults, to say, 'Inasmuch as the peoples of the Ancient Latins have been guilty of wrong against the people of Rome, and inasmuch as the people of Rome have ordered that there be war with the Ancient Latins, and the Senate of the Roman people have determined and decreed that there shall be war with the Ancient Latins, therefore I and the people of Rome declare and make war upon the peoples of the Ancient Latins.' With these words he hurled his spear into their territory.

By means of these legalistic precautions 'a kind of progressive incantation affecting the entire territory' was carried out.* Later, from the third century BC on, it was senatorial legates who went to the frontiers bearing a conditional declaration of war that had been ratified by the people at the proposal of the Senate. If their demands were not met, they immediately announced the opening of hostilities.

The Truce

A legitimate war, duly declared according to the rules, could be suspended in various ways (a truce, a treaty, or a capitulation), either by direct agreement between the belligerents, or through arbitration by a third party.

A truce resulted from a decision taken unilaterally but agreed by both parties to stop fighting temporarily (*ekecheiria, anoché* in Greek, *indutiae* in Latin). The duration varied greatly, from a few hours to several years, depending upon its purpose, which sometimes had little to do with the war itself; for example when, in Greece, combatants were invited through heralds to observe a sacred truce during the great panhellenic festivals. In most cases, however, the belligerents themselves decided to cease fighting in order to celebrate a local feast day, to bury their dead, to exchange prisoners, or above all, to open peace negotiations. The decision came either from the official bodies or,

* G. Dumézil, in Revue des Études Latines 34 (1956) p. 106.

more directly, from those confronting each other on the battle-field. In the latter case the truce was ratified by the army leaders on their own responsibility, at the risk of being disowned by the state they represented.

The Treaty

The treaty (*syntheke* or *spondai* in Greek, *foedus* in Latin), as opposed to the truce, brought a conflict to a genuine end. In Rome its duration was perpetual, but in Greece, until about 375 BC, only for an agreed period, at most a century, with every possibility for a periodic review of the clauses of the agreement at the request of the interested parties. Treaties also differed from truces in that they were necessarily official. They always had to be accepted by the public authorities competent to deal with international affairs and ratified by the representatives of the state specially accredited for this purpose. Furthermore, they were either bilateral or multilateral, even when the parties were obviously unequal in strength. In every case the parties signed a single agreement with the full authority of their 'legal personality.'

Finally, the ratification of treaties was surrounded by legal and religious guarantees of a scope generally greater than was the case when a truce was concluded. Such were, for example, the formalities of the Peace of Nicias which brought the first part of the Peloponnesian War to an end in 421 BC :

> The Athenians and the Spartans and their allies made a treaty (*spondai*) and swore to it, city by city, as follows:
> . . . 'The treaty shall be binding for fifty years upon the Athenians and upon the Spartans and the allies of the Spartans, without fraud or hurt by land or sea . . . The Athenians shall take oaths to the Spartans and their allies, city by city. Every man shall swear by the most binding oath of his country, seventeen from each city. The oath shall be as follows: 'I will abide by this agreement and treaty honestly and without deceit.' In the same way an oath shall be taken by the Spartans and their allies to the Athenians; and the oath shall be renewed annually by both parties. Pillars shall be erected at Olympia, Delphi, the Isthmus, at Athens on the Acropolis, and at Sparta in

51

the temple at Amyclae. If anything be forgotten, whatever it be and on whatever point, it shall be consistent with their oath for both parties, the Athenians and the Spartans, to alter it according to their discretion.' (Thucydides, V, 18.)

According to Livy (I, 24, 3–9), the *foedus* was based on the same principles. He is describing the agreement reached between Rome and the Albans before the battle between the Horatii and the Curatii took place (although the ceremonial is somewhat archaic):

This is the earliest treaty recorded, and as all treaties, however different the conditions they contain, are concluded with the same forms, I will describe the forms with which this one was concluded as handed down by tradition. The *fetial* put the formal question to Tullus: 'Do you, King, order me to make a treaty with the Pater Patratus of the Alban nation?' On the king replying in the affirmative, the *fetial* said: 'I demand of you, King, some tufts of grass.' The king replied, 'Take those that are pure.' The *fetial* brought pure grass from the Citadel. Then he asked the king: 'Do you constitute me the plenipotentiary of the people of Rome, sanctioning also my vessels and comrades?' To which the king replied, 'So far as may be without hurt to myself and the people of Rome, I do.'

The *fetial* was M. Valerius. He made Spurius Furius the Pater Patratus by touching his head and hair with the grass. Then the Pater Patratus, who is constituted for the purpose of giving the treaty the religious sanction of an oath, did so by a long formula in verse, which it is not worth while quoting. After reciting the conditions he said: 'Hear, O Jupiter, hear! thou Pater Patratus of the Alban people! Hear ye too, Alban people: As these conditions have been publicly rehearsed from first to last, from these tablets in perfect good faith, and in as much as they have here and now been most clearly understood, so the people of Rome will not be the first to go back from these conditions. If they shall, in their national council, with false and malicious intent, be the first to go back, then do thou, Jupiter, on that day, so smite the people of Rome, even as I here and now shall smite this swine, and smite them so

much more heavily as thou art greater in power and might.'
With these words he struck the swine with a flint. In similar wise the Albans recited their oath and formularies
through their own dictator and their priests.

The Surrender

Unless one of the adversaries deliberately decided to wage
war until the opponent was totally exterminated, the conquered
were always able, in the last resort, to avoid being wiped out,
by appealing to the mercy of the victor, by capitulating. In
Greece an agreement (*homologia*) was then made, which consisted of stipulations sanctioned by an exchange of oaths.

The Romans regulated such affairs by the procedure of
deditio. Clearly of primitive origin, *deditio* was sufficiently
flexible in its application to be used in many circumstances: it
became a favourite Roman instrument in its expansionist policy.
Formally it was a verbal contract, an early example of which is
recorded by Livy (I, 38, 2) in his account of the surrender of
Collatia to Tarquin the Elder:

> The king asked: 'Have you been sent as envoys and com-
> missioners by the people of Collatia to make the surren-
> der of yourselves and the people of Collatia?' 'We have.'
> 'And are the people of Collatia an independent people?'
> 'They are.' 'Do you surrender into my power and that of
> the people of Rome yourselves, and the people of Collatia,
> your city, lands, water, boundaries, temples, sacred vessels,
> all things divine and human?' 'We do surrender them.'
> 'Then I accept them.'

The act of *deditio* was one of total and unconditional submission, even where preliminary conditions had been settled by
mutual agreement. The victor held an unlimited power similar
to that resulting from the rights of conquest. He made no undertakings at all, whether the surrenderer gave himself up to the
conquerors' will (*deditio in dicionem*) or to his good faith
(*deditio in fidem*), for neither of these two different terms had
any legal force. Whatever the previous position of strength between the two parties, the *deditio* was unaffected by whether it
was offered of one's own accord, or because of threats by the
adversary or through fear of a third party. The fundamental

reason is that the *deditio* removed not only the will of the surrenderer but also, in a sense, his personality. Hence it cannot be considered as a treaty, nor did it involve any oaths. The conqueror was no longer dealing with a person.

However, what he had thus annihilated he could of his own free will recreate: it was always permissible for him to restore the surrenderer's personality, and to bind himself to the surrenderer by a bilateral agreement of one sort or another. The *deditio* thus provided the Romans with infinite legal possibilities for extending their power, ranging from the annihilation of the legal personality to total emancipation of the defeated and including assimilation or the establishment of bonds of friendship, subjection or alliance.

The Guarantees

The implementation of these various types of agreement which suspended military operations or brought the war to a definite end could not be left to the good will of the parties concerned. Guarantees, both real and formal, were necessary.

The real guarantees when they were provided, consisted in the surrender either of material goods (money, harvests, arms) or, more frequently, of hostages. If the agreements had been concluded on an equal footing, hostages were sometimes exchanged by both sides; if not, only by the party suing for peace. In either case there was agreement concerning their number, their social standing and the length of their detention. The latter lasted until all the clauses of the agreement had been fulfilled —unless the vanquished managed to persuade the conqueror to free them earlier or to allow them to be replaced periodically.* By selecting the replacements from progressively lower social groups it was then possible to reduce the value of the guarantees left in the hands of the conqueror. If the agreements were violated, the conqueror could treat the hostages as prisoners of war or do what he wished with them. The Greeks and Romans resorted to this procedure especially in times of insecurity and in their dealings with barbarian peoples.

It was also necessary to ensure publicity, in the case of treaties by depositing them in the public archives and by transcribing

* The earliest known reference to replacement is in an Athenian decree concerning Chalcis soon after the middle of the fifth century B.C.

them on stone pillars placed in the most frequently visited sanctuaries. However, this is not what made international agreements binding. Nor was it the recognition, at least tacit, of any particular ethnic, political or cultural community, as is proved by the fact that all agreements whether concluded with Latin or non-Latin, Italic or non-Italic peoples, held the same value in the eyes of the Romans. What then was the chief factor in making international agreements binding? It was the universal belief in the inviolability of oaths and other forms of commitment to the gods. So it was that the gods were introduced as a third party in agreements concluded between men: a bipartite relationship was converted into a three-sided contract by the intervention of sacred powers.

Most international agreements, particularly treaties, were sanctioned by the oaths of the contracting parties, first at the moment of ratification, occasionally also at regular intervals in the following years. Now an oath sworn by the ancients was not simply a matter of words; something else was needed to sanctify it, to create the power which would punish every failure to fulfil the vow. It was a promise accompanied by a curse and by some gesture which magically symbolised the punishment for perjury, either a libation (*spondai* in Greek, *sponsio* in Latin), so that the guilty one would see his life 'spilt out upon the ground like this wine', to repeat a Homeric phrase (*Iliad* III, 300), or else a blood sacrifice, whereby the slaughtered animal foreshadowed the fate in store for the perjurer.* In this way the guilty man fell under the curse of the gods; he became accursed (*enages* in Greek, *sacer* in Latin). To avoid contamination, the community to which he belonged had to purify itself, or even expel him from its midst by handing him over to the enemy. Such a *deditio* could fall either upon any member of a community bound by an official treaty or just on those who had sworn on their own behalf. In the latter case the Romans entrusted the duty of expulsion to one of the *fetiales*.

Behind all international agreements, whether accompanied by oaths or not, and at the base of the procedure for unconditional surrender lay, ultimately, the concept of 'good faith'

---

* By an extension of meaning, the names of these operations came to be applied to the agreements themselves.

(*pistis* in Greek, *fides* in Latin). It was this in the final analysis that guaranteed a faithful interpretation of the agreement. 'Good faith' was not originally felt to be a secular moral obligation. *Pistis* and *fides* (both derived from the same Indo-European root) appear first to have meant the 'flow of power' which naturally resided in the right hand and gave the possessor overriding authority which would increase or diminish according to how it was used.

Such was the ultimate foundation of international relations in antiquity, in Greece and, above all, in Rome. The Romans considered themselves to be the people of *fides* par excellence, the people who understood the value of an oath and respected it. The founding of the cult of Fides as a divinity was attributed to Numa Pompilius, and as early as 274 BC, the Greek city of Locri, in southern Italy, expressed gratitude to its conquerors by issuing silver coins depicting Rome crowned by Pistis (Fides). This ideology was subsequently much enriched under the influence of Stoic philosophy, at the time of Cicero and Livy, and it retained vitality to the end of the Empire, though assuming an increasingly ethical character which impaired its practical efficacy. It was to this *fides Romana* that the surrenderer in *deditio* made a particular appeal. In exchange for total submission he obtained a double assurance. He set a limit in advance upon the conqueror's powers of action at the same time that he assured himself of the conqueror's protection.

Needless to say, *fides Romana* was as ambiguous in its application as it was strict in theory. But the fact that it provided a convenient moral cover for the deployment of brutal force does not mean that we are dealing with a case of false pretenses, lacking both credibility and effectiveness.

From War to Peace

These guarantees, most of which sprang from the magico-religious matrix which nourished the vital energy of the people of the ancient world, were all the more essential in that the cessation of a war implied not only the end of hostilities but also the establishment of a peaceful relationship involving mutual obligations. Etymologically, the Latin word '*pax*' and possibly also the Greek *eirene*, suggest the 'establishment' of a new state of affairs.

In concluding a peace the differences which had caused the war were indeed settled, the after-effects of the military operations were wound up, and the resulting balance of power was fixed. For instance the defeated party may have been obliged to cede territory, to pay certain contributions, to limit its armaments, to hand over prisoners and deserters, and so on. However, in order that real peace should exist it was furthermore necessary to specify the legal bases for future relations between the former belligerents. In some cases these were established by common agreement, in others they expressed only the will of the conqueror. Except where the conqueror proceeded simply to exterminate or assimilate his adversary, he bound him, as far as he could or wished, by ties of subjection, more or less powerful, more or less apparent. He also bound himself by a treaty of alliance, the advantages of which to the two parties were often unequal. Or at the least he obliged the vanquished to observe neutrality in any conflict with a third party. On occasion, he added further stipulations of a commercial or diplomatic nature.

So in this sense it can be said that the proliferation of wars, between states concerned to define the legal position and to respect their commitments, contributed towards transforming the mere absence of hostilities into a positive peace.

THE LAWS OF WAR

A regular procedure for opening and closing hostilities was but one of the obligations, though essential, which had to be observed by the combatants taking part in a legitimate war. Even in the heat of battle or the intoxication of victory, men at war had to conform to a number of customs aimed, in a general way, at limiting the blind use of force. Though never codified, these customs were widely and correctly enough observed, even in relations with barbarians, for anyone contravening them to be blamed and to have sanctions imposed. The reasons were, in the first instance, religious, but increasingly, as philosophical thought developed, truly humanitarian as well.

The Immunities

The first imperative binding the belligerents equally, even before the balance began to tip in favour of one or the other, was to respect the immunity of anything in any way concerned

57

with the service of the gods. The Greeks were strict upon this point and perhaps more than the Romans took a rigid view of the partisan involvement of national deities in human affairs, and were better equipped with magico-legal devices with which to shed religious scruples with impunity.

In Greece sacrilege was particularly clear and scandalous when it affected the material goods which belonged to the gods (sanctuaries, temples, altars, wealth, flocks and lands) or fell under their protection (tombs, certain types of monuments, sometimes even entire towns). All this went without saying, but it went all the better for being said with maximum publicity. Accordingly, many Greek cities took the precaution of obtaining, particularly from such unscrupulous peoples as the Aetolians or the Cretans, decrees of asylum covering a part or even the whole of their territories. It was so very tempting to plunder the offerings and the accumulated treasures deposited in sanctuaries, to barricade oneself inside a religious building, as the Athenians did at Delium in Boeotia in 424 BC, or to pursue the conquered right into the temples where they dashed for refuge when a city was captured. On such occasions men sometimes forgot the terrible punishment meted out to Ajax by Athena for having brutally torn the prophetess Cassandra from her Trojan temple.

The same immunity applied to all who enjoyed the protection of the gods. Apart from the priests, who for this reason played an important role in diplomatic relations, this category included the soothsayers and sacrificers who accompanied the armies on campaign, the religious ambassadors (*theoroi* and *spondophoroi*), the Dionysiac artists, the competitors and even the spectators in panhellenic games, and other persons who occasionally performed priestly functions, such as the Spartan kings. Others who had equal right to special consideration were those who threw down their arms on the field of battle and presented themselves as suppliants, by kneeling, squatting, sitting on the ground, grasping the knees, chin or right hand of their adversary, or, where the Romans were concerned, by taking refuge near the standards of the legions or the statues of the emperors. But the greatest outrage was to attack the heralds, the 'messengers of Zeus and men'. It was by making a meal of them that the Laestrygonians, in the *Odyssey* betrayed their total savagery;

it was in the memory of the murder of the mythical herald Copreus, it was said, that the Athenian *ephebes* were obliged to wear a black *chlamys*; it was for having killed the Athenian herald Anthemocritus that the Megarians were (according to Pansanias I, 36, 3), condemned by Demeter and Kore to ever-lasting poverty; and we know how difficult it was for the Athenians and Spartans to purge themselves of the murder of the heralds sent by Darius in 491 BC.

As ambassadors gradually superseded the heralds, they in turn came to benefit from a certain personal immunity. It always, however, remained conditional and more or less precarious. As late as 346 BC a special decree of the assembly was necessary each time the Athenians wished to authorise Philip II of Macedon to send them representatives to discuss peace. Besides, the inviolability of ambassadors on mission was frequently ignored by third parties who happened to intercept them.

The fact that the prerogatives were extended to ambassadors bears witness to a certain secularization of international practices. Another step in this direction was the spreading custom of safe-conducts which a military leader, acting either on his own authority or officially, issued to an enemy to enable him to accomplish an exceptional mission. In the end, however, whether these privileges were based on religion, custom, or contract, people felt no hesitation in abusing them if it suited their book. For instance Xenophon tells us (*Hellenica*, IV, 7, 2–3), that in 388 the Spartan king Agesipolis

> went to Olympia and consulted the oracle of the god, asking whether it would be consistent with piety if he did not acknowledge the holy truce claimed by the Argives; for, he urged, it was not when the appointed time came, but when the Spartans were about to invade their territory, that they pleaded the sacred months. And the god signified to him it was consistent with piety for him not to acknowledge a holy truce which was pleaded unjustly. Then Agesipolis proceeded straight from there to Delphi and asked Apollo in his turn whether he also held the same opinion as his father, Zeus, in regard to the truce. And Apollo answered that he did hold quite the same opinion.

Both gods and men in Greece knew how to keep a sense of proportion on the subject of immunity and their eye to the main chance. In 424 BC, after the Delium affair, the Athenians argued this way:

> . . . anything done under the pressure of war and danger might reasonably claim indulgence even in the eyes of the god; or why, pray, were the altars the asylum for involuntary offences? Transgression also was a term applied to presumptuous offenders, not to the victims of adverse circumstances (Thucydides IV, 98, 6).

The Victory

The crucial moment when these prohibitions were most likely to be transgressed was that of victory. For the rights of the conqueror in antiquity were as ambiguous as the duties of the combatants, that is, they were theoretically absolute but vague and limited in application.

Because victory could determine social and political standing it could not be equivocal. It was the result of a categorical judgment of a quasi-divine nature, not open to dispute. Hence certain criteria of victory were required which would permit a firm decision even in the most doubtful situations, when neither side would admit defeat. The most generally used criterion was control of terrain, whether of the battlefield (on land or sea) or of the territory of the state. The defeated side was the one which had abandoned the place of combat, even if his forces were still superior to those of the enemy. (We may again refer to Herodotus' anecdote about the battle between the three hundred Argives and three hundred Spartans for possession of Thyreae.) In siege warfare, if the besieged party would not leave their walls to protect their territory, the aggressor, even if unable to take the city, could claim a 'moral' victory.

When, from the Hellenistic period onwards, military operations became increasingly complex and virulent, the combatants sometimes found good reasons for evading these rather simple criteria which had generally met with approval in the confrontations between city-states. It now became more common for both sides simultaneously to claim victory. At the same time people were beginning to appreciate the relativity of victory, its costs and consequences. They spoke of a 'Pyrrhic' victory recalling the expensive, and in the long run, ruinous exploits of the king of Epirus in Italy.

Burial of the Dead

On the day following a battle the combatants had to fulfil one first, sacred duty; they had to make sure the dead were buried. The conqueror was consequently obliged to respect enemy corpses (once they had been stripped of their arms and any precious objects), and, without waiting for a definitive outcome to the conflict, grant a truce permitting the vanquished to gather up their dead. In the most ancient times this custom appears to have had its violations. In the *Iliad,* both Trojans and Achaeans in certain circumstances proceeded quite shamelessly to mutilate fallen enemy leaders (while the gods, on the contrary, strove to preserve them from corruption), and in the Theban epic there is the example of Theseus who had to launch a campaign against Creon in order to compel him to return the bodies of the seven companions of Polyneices lying at the gates of the city. But by the classical period the Greeks forbade such outrages even when they were dealing with barbarians, as did the Romans ever since the distant time when Aeneas had granted a burial truce to King Latinus.

As a rule, the dead were buried collectively on the battlefield itself, under mounds such as the one which can still be seen today at Marathon. Athens was an exception: according to an 'ancestral law' (*patrios nomos*) earlier than 464 BC, the normal procedure was the following, described by Thucydides (II, 34, 2–6):

> Three days before the ceremony, the bones of the dead are laid out in a tent which has been erected, and their friends bring to their relatives such offerings as they please. In the funeral procession cypress coffins are borne in cars, one for each tribe, the bones of the deceased being placed in the coffin of their tribe. Among these is carried one empty bier for the missing, that is for those whose bodies could not be recovered. Any citizen or stranger who pleases joins in the procession, and the female relatives are there to wail at the burial; with the exception of those slain at Marathon,

who for their singular and extraordinary valour were in-
terred on the spot where they fell. After the bodies have
been laid in the earth, a man chosen by the state, of approved wisdom and eminent reputation, pronounces over
them an appropriate panegyric; after which all retire.

Stone tablets bearing the names of the victims and commem-
orative epigrams concerning their exploits were then set up on
these collective tombs (*polyandria*) in the Keramaikos, a quarter
north-west of the city walls.*

Trophies

Once the dead were buried, if the conqueror wished to ensure
the legitimacy of his victory, to sanction the new order which
resulted, he had to perform a number of rites, religious in origin
but later transformed into honorific privileges of a more or less
secular nature. He began by erecting a trophy on the very site
of the battle. Trophies were originally conceived as prophy-
lactic monuments, in other words as repositories of supernatural
power which helped during the battle but which had to be
neutralised once hostilities had come to an end. They were
therefore made only of perishable materials, so that when they
disappeared the dangerous elements shut up within them would
fade too. Simple pieces of armour were hung on tree trunks,
representing a collective exorcism in which were perhaps fused
primitive cults of both trees and sacred arms. This custom made
its appearance in Attica shortly before the Persian wars, and
spread widely during the fifth century throughout the Greek
world, even to Sparta, where it had earlier been forbidden by a
law attributed to Lycurgus. The culmination came in the Peloponnesian War, with its 'trophymania'.

Meanwhile the appearance as well as the significance of the
trophy was undergoing a change. The tendency was to transform
it into a monument commemorating the glory of the people, and
later of the victorious leader. It was placed under the special
protection of Zeus Tropaios, and it was increasingly affected by
the growing cult of Victory. This development started off right
after the Persian wars, in which the conquered were only bar-

* The generals in command of the Athenian fleet victorious in the battle
of Arginusae in 406 paid with their lives for neglecting to gather up the
battle victims.

barians. In about 460, columns were set up at Marathon (and probably also on the banks of the straits of Salamis), surmounted by a trophy-bearing Victory (*Nike Tropaiophoros*) and these, too, were soon called trophies. However, it was not until 371, at Leuctra, that the first permanent trophy was built, to commemorate a victory of Greeks over Greeks. It was a circular construction, decorated with arms sculpted in bas-relief, a motif which soon won great popularity. In 319 the Athenians copied it on one of their city gates, and it even became a stereotype for the minor arts.

In primitive times, the Romans like the Greeks and certain barbarian peoples were content to burn the enemy spoils on the spot, dedicating them to such gods as Jupiter, Mars, Vulcan and Hercules. Their ideas about 'the sacredness of battle' and the dangers of contamination were evidently much the same as those of the Greeks. Then, by the third century BC, they had no difficulty in adopting, by a kind of osmosis, the device of the trophy, but in their own particular way: they preferred trophies which they could carry in procession or which could be set up on the Capitol, rather than trophies set up on the field of battle.

Then, from the beginning of the first century BC, an evolution set in which continued to the end of the Empire. The trophy was tending to lose its historical and topical character and to become the banal symbol of the victorious power, universal and abstract, which Sulla, Pompey, Caesar and all the emperors believed they possessed. Its position had even less connection with the battlefield than in the past. The trophy set up by Pompey in the Pyrenees after his victories over Sertorius and 'eight hundred and eight-six Iberian tribes', was the first of a series of 'frontier trophies' of which the monument at Adamklissi in Rumania, erected in the reign of Trajan, is an outstanding example. The decoration also became increasingly symbolic. The arms depicted on the trophies rarely pretended to any realism; they aimed rather at evoking, in a very general way, the idea of victory over the most dangerous of human enemies (for instance, Amazons, Galatians and Celts).

From now on, in sum, the trophy was a symbol of the power of the conqueror in its essence and its full glory, and consequently a symbol of his person rather than of his actions. Thus, by the time of Caesar, it was held to be the image of the dictator himself, inhabited by his 'genius', while Augustus went so far as to set himself up as the 'trophy' god *par excellence,* who procured victory and to whom monuments of this kind should therefore be dedicated. As a result, during the whole of the Empire the popularity of trophies and their form depended upon the Imperial ideology as much as upon the military exploits of the emperors. Finally, from the third century on, the trophy as a symbol of eternal and universal Victory, was set up not so much to celebrate successes that had been won, however vague they might be, as to promote future happiness by magical means. This was what allowed the Christians to assimilate it and associate it with the Cross, symbol of the 'genius' of Christ. Having been first dissociated from the vicissitudes of victory, and then from the victorious career of the leader, the trophy had thus, after a thousand years, recaptured something of the magical and impersonal quality which it had possessed at its origins.

Because the trophy had acquired wider significance, it is not surprising that, from the end of the Republic, it tended to lose its architectural originality, although there was an occasional exception, as in the Adamklissi monument, a round tower with three levels. The base was decorated with bas-reliefs, and it rose to a height of 32 metres, crowned with a trophy figuring barbarian captives. This type of representation was henceforth more often to be found on other triumphal monuments: arches, fountains, altars, lighthouses, funeral monuments. Their multiplicity and diversity defy even cursory consideration here.

Thus, in all its various forms throughout antiquity the trophy never ceased to be the embodiment of the energy that produced victory, whether its purpose was to conjure up, celebrate or promote military success, whether it was dedicated to anonymous supernatural powers, to the lords of Olympus, whether it promoted individual charisma, supported the imperial ideology or ensured eternal salvation.

Dedications

The custom of dedicating part of the fruits of victory to a god was based upon similar conceptions to those which justified the practice of putting up trophies. The nature and value of votive offerings placed in Greek sanctuaries varied considerably. Sometimes they bore the generic name of *aparchē* or *akrothimia* (first fruits), sometimes the specific name of *dekatē* (tithe) if they represented one tenth of the booty. They might consist simply of goods which had belonged to the conqueror or to the conquered (helmets and shields as a general rule, as shown by the finds at Olympia and Delphi), or occasionally the rams of warships and war machines. These instruments of war were often supplemented by a share of the proceeds received from selling the booty, sometimes in cash, but usually in prestigious works of art, statues and monuments, for the greater glory of the god and his intrepid worshippers. Warfare was thus the main source of the artistic treasures which accumulated in Greek sanctuaries in the course of centuries.

The practice of offering a tithe was introduced relatively late in Rome, apparently by Camillus in 391 BC, after the capture of Veii, in a dedication to Pythian Apollo. As a general rule a god received a share of the total booty only if the general in command had vowed it in the hour of danger. It was then his duty to ensure that this part of the booty, known as the *manubiae*, was well used. But the Romans preferred an offering of arms and other spoils stripped from the enemy dead to this type of dedication. The most glorious were the *spolia opima*, taken from the person of the enemy leader. There were three types of spoils; the first offered to Jupiter Feretrius, the second to Mars, the third to Janus Quirinus, accompanied by the sacrifice respectively, of a bull, *solitaurilla* (presumably a boar, a ram and a bull), and a lamb.

Because of the prestige attached to them, dedications were often the subject of disputes between cities or between individuals of the same city. After a victory won together, allies would vie with each other for the honour of providing them; for example, shortly after the end of the Peloponnesian War the Spartans turned against the Thebans because, Xenophon explains in the *Hellenica* (III, 5, 5) 'they had long been angry with them . . . on account of their claiming Apollo's tenth at Decelea.'

It was therefore necessary to settle this question peacefully in advance. In the treaty concluded about 450 BC between the Cretan cities of Cnossus and Tylissus, it was stipulated that the men of Cnossus would be responsible for the tithe from captures made in common; the best of the spoils would be sent to Delphi by both parties acting in common, and the rest would be dedicated to Ares at Cnossus by both parties acting in common.*

The Roman Triumph

In Rome, an important enough victory gave the right to hold a triumph. This ceremony went back to the origins of the city; it was said to have been introduced by Romulus, in honour of Jupiter Feretrius, after his victory over the Alban leader, Acron.

It is difficult to be precise about the primitive significance and form; it was probably part of the ritual cycle of consecration and deconsecration which as we have seen provided the framework for the season of war. However, it continued to evolve, in both form and spirit, in order to fulfil the new aspirations of the victorious people. The formal content altered considerably between the end of the sixth century BC and the beginning of the fourth, under the influence of the Etruscans. Thereafter it was addressed to Jupiter Optimus Maximus, and it became increasingly lavish and hierarchic, almost choreographic, while the emphasis came inevitably to be placed upon the individuality and personality of the *triumphator*. A kind of climax appears to have been reached by the end of the third century, by Scipio Africanus after his victory over Carthage :

All who were in the procession wore crowns. Trumpeters led the advance and wagons laden with spoils. Towers were borne along representing the captured cities, and pictures showing the exploits of the war; then gold and silver coin and bullion, and whatever else they had captured of that kind; then came the crowns that had been given to the general as a reward for his bravery by cities, by allies or by the army itself. White oxen came next, and after them elephants and the captive Carthaginian and Numidian chiefs. Lictors clad in purple tunics preceded the general; also a chorus of harpists and pipers, in imitation of an Etruscan procession, wearing belts and golden crowns, and

* *Die Staatsverträge des Altertums*, vol. II, ed. H. Bengtson, No. 148, lines 7–11.

they marched in regular order, keeping step with song and dance. They are called Lydi because, as I think, the Etruscans were a Lydian colony. One of these, in the middle of the procession, wearing a purple cloak reaching to the feet and golden bracelets and necklace, caused laughter by making various gesticulations, as though he were dancing in triumph over the enemy.

Next came a number of incense burners, and after them the general himself on a chariot embellished with various designs, wearing a crown of gold and precious stones, and dressed, according to the fashion of the country, in a purple toga inwoven with golden stars. He bore a sceptre of ivory, and a laurel branch which is always the Roman symbol of victory. Riding in the same chariot with him were boys and girls, and on the trace horses on either side of him young men, his own relatives. Then followed those who had served him in the war as secretaries, aids and armour bearers. After these came the army arranged in squadrons and cohorts, all of them crowned and carrying laurel branches, the bravest of them bearing their military prizes. They praised some of their captains, derided others, and reproached others; for in a triumph everybody is free, and is allowed to say what he pleases. When Scipio arrived at the Capitol the procession came to an end, and he entertained his friends at a banquet in the temple, according to custom.

All that is missing in this description by Appian (VIII, 9, 66) is the episode of the final sacrifice and the public slave who, it is said, murmured throughout the ceremony in the ear of the *triumphator*, 'Remember that you are mortal.'

After a while, however, the triumph was no longer essentially a reward granted by the Senate or people to the victorious general. Its military justification was reduced as it became simply an instrument of political prestige. In the Empire it became the Emperor's privilege, while the actual conqueror received at best some triumphal ornaments or the right to an ovation (possibly the original form of the triumph). Under arches specially erected for the occasion there were now processions of various types, more colourful under Nero, Domitian and the emperors of the third century, more subdued in the reigns of Augustus, Trajan or Diocletian.

Thus conceived, the triumph could be transformed at will to serve the prevailing ideology; it reappears in the Byzantine Empire, and later in ecclesiastical ceremony dedicated to the glory of the *triumphator in excelsis,* and even in our own time in manifestations as widely differing in their purpose as the papal coronation, the New Orleans carnival, and the 'popular' processions along the Champs-Elysées.

The Imperator

During the last years of the Republic a victorious general, even when he did not obtain a triumph, could hope that the Senate would decree days of public prayer (*supplicationes*) in his honour, as indeed he might expect his soldiers, duly primed, to take the initiative in hailing him as *imperator*. This latter practice, inaugurated in Spain at the end of the third century for Scipio Africanus, did not at first confer any official title upon its hero. It simply confirmed, in all solemnity, the victory and the natural aptitude for command of the man who had been instrumental in mobilising the troops (if this is indeed the primitive meaning of the word). Gradually, however, generals acquired the habit of mentioning this honorary distinction together with their other titles, and it tended increasingly to become institutionally integrated and to merge with the official titles of the *cursus* (official career). From the time of Sulla this development speeded up, so Octavian (Augustus) felt able to use the word as a title preceding his name, although its legal meaning was not specified. Again adopted by Nero, then by Vespasian and his successors, *imperator* came to designate the man who possessed supreme power, especially since the emperors ensured themselves a monopoly of military acclamations.

The Rights of Conquest

Provided he had satisfied the concluding religious obligations and provided there was no prior agreement narrowing the consequences of defeat, the victor automatically enjoyed absolute and unconditional rights of property over the fruits of victory. The unanimity in antiquity on this score is exemplified by the following statements:

THE LEGAL ASPECTS OF ANCIENT WAR

Xenophon (*Cyropaedia* VII, 5, 73): '. . . it is a law established for all time among all men that when a city is taken in war, the persons and the property of the inhabitants belong to the captors.'

Plato (*Republic* V 468A): '. . . if any fall alive into the enemies' hands we shall make them a present of him, and they may do what they like with their prey . . .'; (*Laws* I 626B): '. . . all the goods of the vanquished fall into the hands of the victors.'

Aristotle (*Politics* 1255a6–7): '. . . those vanquished in war are held to belong to the victor . . .'

Livy (XXXIV, 57, 7), reporting the intervention of an ambassador of Antiochus III before the Roman Senate: '. . . conditions were dictated to those who had been vanquished in war, for when everything had been surrendered to the one who was the stronger in arms he had the absolute right to say what they might retain and of what they were to be deprived.'

The fruits of victory thus included all the persons as well as the goods. And the Romans, more frequently than the Greeks, also included the gods, unless the gods, more opportunistic than their devotees, had already responded to the *evocatio* from the enemy camp before the hour of defeat had struck. The victor could either condemn them to death, so to speak, by depriving them of offerings, prayers and sacrifices, or he could lead them into captivity in order to enrich his own pantheon, no matter how alien they were to him. According to Arnobius (III, 38), the Romans generally divided this special type of booty into two parts: one was distributed as private property among the great Roman families, the rest was assigned to public cults, sometimes under the supervision of the family of the victorious general.

Livy (V, 22, 3–7) describes such a transfer of gods after the capture of the Etruscan city of Veii:

> When all that belonged to man had been carried away from Veii, they began to remove from the temples the votive gifts that had been made to the gods, and then the gods themselves; but this they did as worshippers rather than as plunderers. The deportation of Queen Juno to Rome was entrusted to a body of men selected from the whole army, who after performing their ablutions and arraying

69

themselves in white vestments, reverently entered the temple and in a spirit of holy dread placed their hands on the statue, for it was as a rule only the priest of one particular house who, by Etruscan usage, touched it. Then one of them, either under sudden inspiration or in a spirit of youthful mirth, said 'Art thou willing, Juno, to go to Rome ?' The rest exclaimed that the goddess nodded assent. An addition was made to the story to the effect that she was heard to say, 'I am willing.' At all events we have it that she was moved from her place by appliance of little power, and proved light and easy of transport, as though she was following of her own accord. She was brought without mishap to the Aventine, her everlasting seat, whither the prayers of the Roman dictator had called her, and where this same Camillus afterwards dedicated the temple which he had vowed.

It was particularly characteristic of the Romans that traces of the juristic conception of the rights of conquest were to be found, even at quite a late date, in certain civil formalities for transmitting property—for example a sale by auction was *sub hasta,* 'under the lance'—and in certain institutional procedures which for a long time continued to be conceived as simulated combats.

The discretionary powers of the victor over the possessions of the conquered gave him the right either to destroy them or to preserve them for his own profit, if that was in his best interest (and if he was capable of appreciating this fact in the heat of battle). However, in some cases destruction incurred a certain measure of moral blame. For instance the wanton destruction of fruit trees and domestic animals was always deplored as was that of captured slaves, for not only were their services appreciated but as the centuries passed there was a tendency to adopt an increasingly humanitarian attitude towards them.

In theory conquest eliminated the distinction between slaves and free men. Upon falling into the enemy's hands they were all deprived of their previous status. What became of them? From a legal point of view they were just so many individuals at the mercy of the enemy like the rest of the booty. No status resembling that of the modern prisoner of war was granted to them. Hence there was no specific word with which to designate them. In both Greek and Latin the same words could be used for both men and goods in the power of the enemy. There were several such terms, alluding to the circumstances of their capture or to the fate reserved for them, all of which shows that the men had reality in the eyes of their masters only as captives.

In practice, there were three possibilities open to the victor. He could put them to death, reduce them to slavery or liberate them, more or less gratuitously, after a period of detention. They might be put to death the moment they were captured in the heat of battle or in the frenzy of sacking a besieged city. (In the latter case the entire population was usually affected, less often a particular category.) But it also happened in cold blood, sooner or later after their capture, and for various reasons (as human sacrifices in archaic times, or on account of the conqueror's anger, or as an act of reprisal). The *Iliad* and *Odyssey* bear witness to an age when men were put to death without such scruple: this would explain why men slaves were apparently less numerous in Homeric society (29 examples) than women (51 examples), whose skills were more highly valued. With the passing of time the execution of prisoners lost the quasi-ritual character that it had in the primitive societies, probably founded upon economic necessities. In Rome, the change was completed by 264 BC, when, under the influence of Lucania and Campania prisoners of war were transformed into gladiators, giving them a chance of saving their lives. Throughout antiquity, however, the ancient practices were still resorted to frequently enough in moments of anger or as punishment for 'treachery' or 'impiety'.

In Greece enslavement of captives does not appear to have been more common than massacre—one quarter of the recorded cases. However it would be wrong to pay too much attention to this calculation and so to minimise the role of war as a source of slaves; unlike massacre, enslavement often affected entire populations, not just the fighting men. In Homeric times that was the normal practice: those who were spared remained in the personal service of their conqueror. There are still many instances of this from the classical period too, chiefly

in wars between Greeks and Barbarians. The captives, sometimes branded, were sold on the market or assigned to forced
labour, especially in the mines. However, by the end of the
classical period such procedures began to be condemned as too
harsh, except, once again, in the case of barbarians. Among civi-
lised men, Romans as well as Greeks, it was henceforth considered proper to liberate prisoners after a certain length of
time, so long, that is, as the practice fitted in with the politics of
Roman territorial expansion.

The Release of Captives

The conditions of liberation varied. When peace was the
result of a compromise, there was an exchange of prisoners. If
the conquered party capitulated or made a treaty on an unequal footing his prisoners alone were returned, immediately
the war ended. The victor could then do as he liked with his
prisoners. For obvious reasons he usually sought to derive the
maximum profit from their release: if the prisoners were mercenaries he might enrol them in his own forces, otherwise he
expected a ransom.

The price of ransom varied according to the social condition
of those involved, the political situation in general, and the
state of the slave market.

The very fact that they were captives usually made it impossible for prisoners to pay for their liberty. Someone else
therefore had to assume the responsibility, in archaic societies
often the kinsmen. A law of Gortyn in Crete of about 460 BC
imposed an obligation on Gortynians to buy back members of
their *hetairia* who were put up for sale by the enemy. Later the
state itself, with that heightened sense of collective solidarity
which inspired it in early times, sometimes intervened directly
(as in Rome, during the second Punic war). Alternatively, a
semi-public organ for mutual aid, like the church in the late
Empire, performed this function. Between allied or friendly
peoples the subject was, on occasion incorporated in a treaty.
For instance, in about 260 BC such a treaty was drawn up between Miletus and the Cretan cities of Cnossus, Gortyn and
Phaestus. And at all times, men turned to those who felt a
vocation, more or less altruistic, for the role of benefactor
(*euergetes*). Increasingly, however, with the decline of family

solidarity, of mutual help between citizens and of the spirit of 'euergetism', it became necessary to depend upon the non-benevolent intervention of individuals.

In theory, a man whose rights and personality had been in suspension while he was in captivity should have automatically recovered his old status the moment he set foot on his native soil. The Romans spoke of the right of *postliminium* which restored to the 'living dead' his former condition, his possessions and his family. (Not until the time of Constantine was a woman who was unable to prove the death of her husband in captivity prohibited from remarrying.) But in fact things did not always work out this way, either because the repatriated man had first to prove he had been honourably captured, and then returned to his country, or, as was more often the case, because he had first to repay the ransom advanced in his name by an intermediary. In such cases the ancients took considerable pains to safeguard the interests of both parties. Both in Greece and in the Roman Empire from the end of the second century to the fourth a 'man brought back from the enemy' belonged to his 'benefactor' as a slave, until the ransom was repaid. The Gortyn code expressly stipulated that a free man ransomed from a foreigner 'will be at the disposal of the man who bought him until he has repaid what he owes', and in both Greece and Rome the extinction of this obligation was sanctioned by a form of manumission. This type of slave was, however, of a very particular kind: he engaged his services without abandoning either his personality or his patrimony. He lost his independence but not his liberty. At other times, under the Roman Republic and at the beginning of the Empire, it even seems that ransom was juristically assimilated into the law of debt, not of sale. These varied measures rested on the twofold desire to respect the native liberty of a citizen on his own territory and, in terms of the international situation, to encourage the practice of buying back prisoners of war. The guarantees given to the buyer were increased or diminished according to the gravity of the problems which such a course presented. On the whole, the fate of prisoners was perhaps ameliorated. But we should be mistaken if we saw this trend as evidence of humanitarian feelings at work or of a growing respect for human personality. Essentially, the motivation was social or political, reflecting the interests of the community rather than of the individual. Hence, when it was in their interest—for example in the conquest of Gaul by Caesar—the Romans easily reverted to the most primitive ways of treating prisoners, untroubled by any scruples.

The Division of the Spoils of War

When the time came to divide the spoils of war (both booty and prisoners), a share was first reserved for the gods. Then a conflict often arose among the soldiers, or they formed common cause against the superior interests of the community, more or less identified with those of the leader or of a social minority. The operation could not, therefore, be left to improvisation, for fear of letting loose anarchy and discord in the ranks of the victor; it had to be controlled by custom, if not by rules. Particular circumstances apart, the variations in these procedures reflect quite faithfully the degree to which the individual soldier was subordinated to the power of the state.

In Homeric Greece, a distinction was drawn between two different kinds of booty. There was the individual prize, the soldier's personal acquisition, and the booty taken individually or collectively which was deposited in the common pool to be shared out. First the 'shares of honour' were allocated, reserved for important personalities who had distinguished themselves in the battle. Then the king performed the distribution according to proportions which are unknown to us but which appear to have enabled him to 'share out little and retain much.'

Later, with the formation of cities and the progress of democracy, social privileges within the army came to be given less weight (although the supplementary benefits allocated to the bravest of the warriors was never abolished). There was thus a tendency both to limit personal booty and to equalize the shares. At the same time, however, the needs of the state, increasingly pressing, stopped all the captured booty from passing into the hands of the soldiers. This new dilemma, also arising in other spheres, for example in Athens, over the use of the profits from the silver mines of Laurium, shortly before the second Persian war, could sometimes lead to violent conflicts.

A particular case in point occurred in Rome, about 400 B.C. It was decided to appoint quaestors in the armies to defend the interests of the state, which, as everyone knew, coincided in this situation with the interests of the senatorial aristocracy. Livy's account of the capture of Veii by Camillus (V, 20) reveals the acuteness of the problem:

When the dictator saw that victory was now within his grasp, that a very wealthy city was on the point of capture, and that there would be more booty than had been amassed in all the previous wars taken together, he was anxious to avoid incurring the anger of the soldiers through too niggardly a distribution of it on the one hand, and the jealousy of the Senate through too lavish a grant of it on the other. He sent a despatch to the Senate in which he stated that, through the gracious favour of heaven, his own generalship, and the persevering efforts of his soldiers, Veii would in a very few hours be in the power of Rome, and he asked for their decision as to the disposal of the booty.

The Senate were divided. It is reported that the aged P. Licinius, who was the first to be asked his opinion by his son, urged that the people should receive public notice that whoever wanted to share in the spoils should go to the camp at Veii. Appius Claudius took the opposite line. He stigmatised the proposed largesse as unprecedented, wasteful, unfair, reckless. If, he said, they thought it sinful for money taken from the enemy to lie in the treasury, drained as it had been by the wars, he would advise that the pay of the soldiers be supplied from that source, so that the plebs might have so much less tax to pay. 'The homes of all would feel alike the benefit of a common boon, the rewards won by brave warriors would not be filched by the hands of city loafers, ever greedy for plunder, for it so constantly happens that those who usually seek the foremost place in toil and danger are the least active in appropriating the spoils.'

Licinius, on the other hand, said that 'this money would always be regarded with suspicion and aversion, and would supply material for indictments before the plebs, and consequently bring about disturbances and revolutionary measures. It was better therefore that the plebs should be conciliated by this gift, that those who had been crushed and exhausted by so many years of taxation should be relieved and get some enjoyment from the spoils of a war in which they had almost become old men. When anyone brings home something he has taken from the enemy with his own hand, it affords him more pleasure and gratification than if he were to receive many times its value at the bidding of another. The dictator had referred the question to the Senate because he wanted to avoid the odium and misrepresentations which it might occasion; the Senate, in its turn, ought to entrust it to the plebs and allow each to keep what the fortune of war has given him.' This was felt to be the safer course, as it would make the Senate popular. Notice was accordingly given that those who thought fit should go to the dictator in camp to share in the plunder of Veii.

As the political framework of the city broke down and democracy declined, there was a tendency for the state to assert its sovereign right to dispose of the spoils of war, especially those which came in monetary form and any profit accruing from the sale of prisoners. The state never, however, succeeded in stopping individual soldiers from retaining prizes, nor in totally suppressing the immediate distribution on the spot of a portion of the collective booty. Indeed the use of mercenaries and the growing militarism of power often left both military leaders and the civilian authorities with little room for manoeuvre in this respect.

The possibilities of conflict were all the more acute in campaigns conducted in common with allies. For this reason, the ancients were careful to regulate in advance the distribution among the allies of the possible spoils of war. Sometimes equal portions were assigned to each of the various participants, as in the treaty of 493 BC between the Romans and the Latins, who were joined eight years later by the neighbouring Hernicii. More frequently the distribution took account of the respective strengths of the forces: hence in the treaty concluded with Cnossus in about 450 BC, the Tylissians found they were allocated only a third of the spoils acquired on land but half of those acquired at sea. The simplest way to make an unequal distribution was to base the ratio on the number of soldiers. That was specifically provided in a Hellenistic Cretan treaty:

If in the course of our common campaign, we by the grace of the gods capture anything belonging to the enemy, let each group of Lyttians and Mallians who have taken part in the expedition receive a share proportional to the number of their men.*

One other method was to distinguish between the movable spoils which included all human captives, and the immovable wealth, the city and its territory. Examples are known throughout the ancient world, particularly in Greece from the beginning of the classical period and in Rome from the fourth century B.C. The best piece of evidence is in the treaty of 212 between the Romans and the Aetolians:

If the Romans take by force certain cities belonging to these communities, let the Roman people allow the Aetolian people to dispose of these cities and territories as they will. If the Romans and Aetolians, acting together, take any of these cities, let the Romans allow the Aetolians to treat these cities and territories as they will. And whatever they capture apart from the cities, let it be held by them in common. If any of these cities come over to the side of the Romans or Aetolians or join them, let the Roman people allow the Aetolians to receive these men, cities and territories into their confederation.†

Thus, in the ancient world, war underwent a process of legal formalisation which distinguished it, as the opposite of peace, from the condition of embryonic hostility in which primitive communities usually existed. To understand this process it is not enough to call upon automatic evolution and the proliferation of conflicts. Before conflicts could emerge from their pre-legal framework the political structure of the communities had to be established: in other words, the concept of the state had to develop internally. Thereafter military and political (state) phenomena reinforced one another. War became institutionalised and, at the same time, imprinted a military character upon state structures.

* *Die Staatsverträge des Altertums*, vol. III, ed. H. H. Schmitt, No. 511, lines 4–8.
† *Inscriptiones Graecae* IX 1², 2, 241 lines 4–21.

2

The Military Societies

In antiquity only a minority of the male population was normally engaged in military operations. The low level of the forces
of production made it impossible for mobilisation to pass a
certain threshold, lower than in modern times, without jeopard-
ising the very existence of the community. Each community
therefore contained within it a military society with carefully
defined limits.

Qualitatively, the military society was always, in law if not
in fact, the social elite in whose hands power lay. The ancient
view was that power was in effect derived from the use of force
and could be maintained only by force. Hence those philosophers who speculated upon the origins of civilisation usually
linked the rise of the military art with the rise of the art of
politics. According to Protagoras, for example, the one was
simply a part of the other; together they ensured the cohesion
of the civic body by enforcing, from within and from without,
the idea of a fair exchange in human relations.* Since ancient
warfare, as we have seen, was determined legally and formally
by the establishment of inter-community relations of a state
type, war as a social practice was the product of changes over
the centuries in the composition of the military societies,
and therefore in the structure of the social organisms as
totalities.

THE MILITARY ROLE OF SLAVES

Before embarking upon a study of this development we should
perhaps examine the military role of slaves.† This will make

---

* Thomas Cole, *Democritus and the Sources of Greek Anthropology* (1967),
pp. 123–6.

† I use the word 'slave' in its widest sense to include all those who were
not considered to be free men, regardless of the legal terms in which the
degree and form (collective or individual) of their bondage was expressed.

it possible to grasp immediately the fundamental significance of the criterion of recruitment just mentioned.

Normally slaves played only a secondary and indirect role in the army. In particular they relieved the fighting men of all the fatigue duties, in other words they performed the same social functions as in civilian life. Only in moments of crisis, when the very existence of the community was in jeopardy were they, or at least some of them, enrolled as soldiers. Sometimes, however, especially in the Roman armies, they were entrusted with whatever weapons happened to be available so that they could guard the baggage during a battle.

As for the Greek navies, the Peloponnesian War appears to have been the principal occasion when they were reduced to manning the oars with slaves, in the Corcyrean and Peloponnesian fleets at the beginning, on the side of the Athenians and their allies in the final stages (in particular in 406 and 404, before the battles of Arginusae and Aegospotami). Other examples are known from the fourth century BC among the Spartans and with certain tyrants such as Dionysius the Elder in Syracuse and Jason of Pherae in Thessaly.

Among the Greeks, half the available evidence for slaves serving in land forces concerns the Spartans. From the First Messenian War (at the end of the eighth century BC) until the reign of Cleomenes III (end of the third century BC) and including the battle of Plataea in 479, helots were called up frequently enough, to serve alongside free men. In all probability the same happened to indigenous populations reduced to collective bondage elsewhere in the Greek world, such as the penestai of Thessaly. In contrast, wherever individual enslavement prevailed, as in Athens, it appears that slaves were called upon only in very exceptional circumstances. Thus, in 490, on the eve of the battle of Marathon, the Athenians decided upon such a course, on the motion of Miltiades, whereas they voted against it in 337 BC, after the defeat of Chaeronea. Several other cities called upon their slaves during the unrelenting Peloponnesian War, and again at the beginning of the Hellenistic period when they were on the point of succumbing to the attacks of Alexander and his successors. In 305, the Rhodians decided: 'to buy from their masters any slaves who proved themselves brave men in battle, and to emancipate and enfranchise them.' (Diodorus, XX, 84, 3.)

In the last throes of resistance to Roman Imperialism the matter again became an order of the day, for the last time. In 146, for example, the Achaean general Diaios 'sent a circular letter to all the cities' of his confederation

> ordering them to set free their slaves who were of military age, and who had been born (*oikogeneis*) and brought up (*paratrophai*) in their houses, and send them, furnished with arms, to Corinth. He assigned the numbers to be furnished by the several cities at random and without any regard to equality, just as he did everything else. Those who had not the requisite number of home-bred slaves were to fill up the quota imposed on each city from other slaves (Polybius, XXXIX, 15, 3–5).

On the other hand, throughout Greek history there are instances of slaves contributing to the defence of the urban settlements and throwing themselves spontaneously into the fighting at their masters' sides. For example, in 431 BC, the Plataeans chased a Theban commando raid from their city with the assistance, as Thucydides notes (II, 4, 2), 'of the women and servants who shrieked and shouted from the houses, hurling stones and tiles.'

These different instances of military collaboration between slaves and free men are only exceptions which in some respects illustrate the strength of the rules:

(1) Usually slaves were given only a subordinate military role (as oarsmen or light infantrymen).

(2) The slaves most frequently called up were from the peoples in collective servitude, such as the Thessalian *penestai* and above all the Laconian helots, the very people who demonstrated their desire to be free most violently in times of war, by flight or by open revolt. This paradox can easily be explained: it was precisely their ancient traditions and their natural yearning to be a free people, repressed only with difficulty, which qualified them to a degree for military service. Among the individual slaves, on the other hand, preference seems to have been given to those who were closest to their masters through their birth, their occupation or their way of life, or, as we have

seen in Achaea, the even smaller group of slaves 'born in the house' or 'brought up with the family'.

(3) When the texts which we possess envisage a reward to the slave-soldiers, it nearly always takes the form of their liberty. In Sparta they were normally freed at the end of the war, having been more or less promised their liberty when they were enrolled. But in most Greek cities the procedure apparently varied according to whether the slaves were called upon to serve in the navy or in the land forces. The former were freed after the campaign, the latter beforehand. Why was this distinction made? Presumably in part for reasons of expediency. Service on land, involving personal commitment, demanded more initiative and consequently more determination than did service at sea, where it was easier to impose collective discipline upon the recruits, who were shackled to their benches. This, however, does not altogether account for the Spartan procedures. We must seek another, ideological explanation. For a slave (in the narrow sense) to be deemed fit to serve in the army, it was first necessary to raise his status, since the ideological gap between his status and the new function he was to fulfil was too great, whereas this was not the case with the slave-oarsman whose function was less honourable, or with the helot-soldier whose original status was anyway higher.

(4) As the centuries passed, it seems that the slave community became more and more directly affected by military operations, and that in times of war their reactions to the free men became increasingly hostile or loyal, as the case may be. One reason presumably is that the distance which separated them, both in theory and practice, tended to become somewhat reduced; another, on the political level, is that the struggle against foreign imperialism, Macedonian and above all Roman, sometimes encouraged awareness of the opposition between masters and slaves, sometimes made unity of action necessary.

Roman ideas were similar to those of the Greeks. In the Republic slaves were exempt from military service, save in quite exceptional circumstances, as during the darkest hours of the Second Punic War when some use was made of those slaves who were most likely to prove loyal. The rule was relaxed in the first century, in the Social War and in the pitiless civil wars among the factions supporting Marius, Sulla, Pompey or

Caesar. But it was soon reestablished by Octavian (Augustus), who held himself up as the restorer of Roman traditions in opposition to Sextus Pompey. In his principate slaves were increasingly eliminated first from the land forces and later from the navy. The exclusion remained in force throughout the Empire as is shown by a letter (X, 30) from Trajan to Pliny the Younger on the subject of two slaves discovered among the recruits in Bithynia in north-western Asia Minor:

> Sempronius Caelianus (a recruiting officer) was carrying out my instructions in sending you the slaves. Whether they deserve capital punishment will need investigation; it is important to know if they were volunteers or conscripts, or possibly offered as substitutes. If they are conscripts, then the blame falls on the recruiting officer; if substitutes, then those who offered them as such are guilty; but if they volunteered for service, well aware of their status, then they will have to be executed. The fact that they were not yet enrolled in a legion makes little difference for the truth about their origin should have come out on the actual day they were accepted for the army.*

The rule that military duties were proportional to social status referred to at the beginning of this chapter can thus be seen to have operated even for slaves. It was a rule which obtained even when, under pressure of circumstances, situations sometimes arose which tended to undermine it. We must now examine the way the rule operated in practice, within communities of free men, in relation to the particular structures.

MILITARY ARISTOCRACIES

Some historians hold that the communities of the Neolithic Age, which are supposed to have shown few marks of internal differentiation, enjoyed a relatively egalitarian democratic regime, such as that revealed as late as the third millennium BC in the Sumerian cities. However, as far back as we can go in the history of the Greek and Italic peoples, we never reach this 'virginal' stage of human evolution (in itself already highly

---

* Freedmen were called upon in exceptional circumstances in the army, and more regularly in the navy, at least under the Republic and Early Empire.

complex). On the contrary, we are always dealing with communities characterised by a division of labour from an economic point of view, more or less strongly hierarchical from a social point of view, and politically subject to monarchical or aristocratic authority (although it is true that here and there, especially among the elementary solidarity groups, there are firmly rooted democratic traditions which we are inclined to see as vestiges of an earlier age).

At the beginning of Greek and Roman history the warrior function does not appear to have been limited to one specialised class within the social body. All that can be observed is a concentration of military capacities and responsibilities at the top of the social hierarchy, in an elite who play a determining role on the field of battle corresponding to its role in political and economic affairs. Power, military glory and wealth all fell to the same minority, while the subordinated masses were caught in a tight network of obligations of service which fixed both the levels of the social hierarchy and their participation in military activities.

Such a process of differentiation had already characterised the organisation of the armed forces in the kingdoms of Cnossus and Pylos at the end of the Mycenaean period. So far as we can tell from the present state of our epigraphic sources, there were two ranks, the anonymous infantry organised into basic groups of ten, and probably recruited on the spot, and the 'officers', who were always referred to by name and who centred round the palace where they received their de luxe equipment. We do not know upon what principles recruitment for these two categories was carried out. There is, however, reason to suppose that the 'officers' came from a permanent aristocracy that was organically, but not exclusively, connected with the profession of arms.

Homer makes a comparable distinction within the fighting force, between an elite obligated publicly to parade its wealth, its power and its courage, and the common people whose main function both in war and in peace, on the battlefield as in the *agora*, appears to have been to group themselves compactly in the background of the historical stage in order to support and applaud the chivalry of the heroes. What had changed in the interval from the fall of Mycenae was the nature of the relationships of subordination on which the social and military hierarchy rested. The Mycenaean state structures, which did not survive the Dorian invasions, had been replaced by other principles of solidarity, which were in some respects 'primitive', binding members of the community together by links of personal dependence based on kinship or patronage, or simply by neighbourhoods.

As for Rome, few traces survive of the system of army recruitment before the so-called Servian reforms. There is, however, little reason to doubt its aristocratic nature. Originally the army included only the patrician elite of landowners. In contrast with the *plebs* these constituted the *populus,* a word which appears to have originally had a specifically military sense.

Warrior Confraternities

The archaic aristocracy often appears to be a group functionally dedicated to the practice of arms. This is suggested by the education and life-style of the Homeric heroes, wholly orientated towards the services of Ares. In Sparta, even well into the classical period, the same orientation is seen among the Equals (*Homoioi*), who, thanks to the helots, did not have to earn a living. Among other practices destined to strengthen the homogeneity and purity of this group, there was the double obligation upon completion of a long training period marked by a series of probationary texts, to take their meals together (*syssitia*), and to pass the night in male dormitories (*andreia*). Presumably the survival of many Greek communities of elite corps specialising in the profession of arms can be similarly explained. One example is the sacred battalion of the Thebans, three hundred strong, whose members went by the archaic labels of *heniochoi* (charioteers) and *paraibatai* (companions). On these analogies we can also understand certain aspects of the Roman military organisation during the early years of the Republic—for instance, the way certain *gentes,* such as the Horatii and the Fabii, specialised in particular military activities; patrician control over the religious, political and technical management of military affairs; the association of the equestrian order with military service; the survival of a strict distinction between the military side and the civilian side of citizenship.

These examples show that the early warrior aristocracy submitted to a particularly strict collective discipline, permitting it simultaneously to improve its military expertise and to confirm its social supremacy. It came to organise itself into confraternities which took over for their own purposes (partly because of their educational value, partly out of attachment to traditional forms of social organisation) certain of the still more primitive initiation rites which fell into disuse among the rest of the population.

However, the fact that war was the main activity of these aristocracies does not prove that war was their only function, even less that war was the primary and determining cause of the process of social differentiation from which they emerged. An agglomeration of classes, each with only a single function, each homogenous and mutually exclusive was to be found neither at Mycenae nor in the times of Homer or Romulus. What we invariably find instead are communities in which, though there was certainly a dominant military force, the warrior as such was not distinguished from the nobleman and the man of wealth. The military power of the aristocracy corresponded to its dominant role in every area, economic, social and political. These communities were therefore not the outcome of a simple process of hierarchical grading among the representatives of different social techniques. And there is no doubt that this was also the case in still earlier times, for anthropology has not produced a single primitive community in which a division into functional castes was the starting-point for communal life, or in which the community survived by disregarding the distribution of social resources.

The formation of the city, which ended by establishing new social relationships in Greece by the eighth century and in Rome in perhaps the fifth century BC, tended to reduce the political privileges of the aristocracy and, at the same time, its military dominance. But this evolution did not destroy the continuity in the history of the warrior function. Rather, the enlarged community of free men steadily assimilated the specific activities of the elite. This, as we shall see later, explains the gradual change in the methods of combat characteristic of these social groups, the transmission, with some modifications, to the whole citizen body of the ethics of military valour which had developed within the warrior confraternities. In Rome, this process of 'normalisation' is often expressed in the narrative of the origins of the Republic by an internal tension within the group of warriors torn between loyalty to their own character and the need to become integrated in the new social order. One case in point is that of Lucius Junius Brutus delivering his city from his uncle Tarquin the Proud, who 'had nothing whatever to make good his claim to the crown except actual violence' (Livy, I, 49, 3). His revolt was directed not against an Etruscan king but rather against a representative of the warrior function for whom the reality of violence, *vis*, led to scorn for social legality, *ius*. Throughout the fifth century BC those who championed traditional morality and were prepared to sacrifice the city to their own *furor* were opposed by others who were willing to subordinate their natural impulses in the overall demands of the new society, to lower their *fasces* before the people or to intervene in order to reconcile the patriciate and the plebs, who often found themselves in functional opposition to each other.

THE CITIZEN–SOLDIER

The city was born in a long process, whereby the natural structures of communities were replaced by a conventional mode of organisation in which the theoretical equality among a larger privileged minority was based on *political* criteria. However, the new political development did not affect the status of the military function as the dominant function of the social elite; it merely broadened the social composition of the warriors. Within the framework of the city, the concepts of soldier and of citizen were not in conflict nor was the extension of the military society and of the political society. We shall see, however, when we study the introduction of hoplite tactics, contemporary with the formation of the city-state, that it is always difficult to pinpoint the motivating forces, whether military or political, which account for the transformation of such a 'historical entity'.

Political Rights and Military Duties

This functional equality was not conceived in terms of rights and duties, as it is in our society with its increasing alienation of the citizen from service to the state. In the ancient city the modern formulation would have had no meaning : rights and duties, in political as in military affairs, were combined to define a single condition, a single behaviour-pattern, an ideological whole, an indivisible network of burdens and privileges which belonged in principle to the citizen-soldier and to him alone.

In practice, to be sure, this harmony was disrupted by exceptional traditions or by the necessities of the hour, and it was in danger of being shattered at any moment by dissolvent forces produced by the city 'despite itself'. However, let us for the moment disregard these irregularities and attempt to define the fundamental correspondence between the citizen and the soldier by analysing it in its components. A citizen was by definition a soldier. This first proposition is, in its general application, so little open to argument (except in the case of incapacity duly recognised by the official organs of the city) that it would seem more illuminating to limit our demonstration to one principle which it entails; namely that the degree of political qualification determined the degree of military qualification. In other words, in both contexts the citizen occupied the same place in the social hierarchy. When military duties were distributed among the various *census* (property) classes the highest classes were assigned the greatest obligations (at least, those which were so judged whatever their effective contribution to the defence of the city).

Thus, in fifth-century Athens, the members of the first *census* class (the *pentacosiomedimnoi*) had the privilege of the trierarchy, the principal liturgy, which made them responsible for manning the fleet. For service in the cavalry, one had to belong at least to the second *census* class (*hippeis*); for the hoplite phalanx, the third class (*zeugites*): while the lowest class, the *thetes*, were restricted to the light infantry. The situation in Rome was similar after the so-called 'Servian reform'. The principles may in fact have been established by a king, Servius Tullius, in the middle of the sixth century BC (but not the details which presuppose the use of coinage from the end of the fourth century BC). A detailed description has been left us by Livy (I, 43, 1–11):

> Those whose property amounted to or exceeded 100,000 copper asses were formed into eighty 'centuries', forty of juniors and forty of seniors. These were called the First

Class. The seniors were to defend the city, the juniors to serve in the field. The armour which they were to provide themselves with comprised helmet, round shield, greaves and coat of mail, all of bronze; these were to protect the person. Their offensive weapons were spear and sword. To this class were attached two centuries of engineers whose duty it was to work the engines of war; they were without arms. The Second Class consisted of those whose property amounted to between 75,000 and 100,000 asses; they were formed, seniors and juniors together, into twenty centuries. Their regulation arms were the same as those of the First Class, except that they had an oblong wooden shield instead of a round bronze one and no coat of mail. The Third Class he formed of those whose property fell as low as 50,000 asses; these also consisted of twenty centuries, similarly divided into seniors and juniors. The only difference in the armour was that they did not wear greaves. In the Fourth Class were those whose property did not fall below 25,000 asses. They also formed twenty centuries; their only arms were a spear and a javelin. The Fifth Class was larger, it formed thirty centuries. They carried slings and stones. . . .

This Fifth Class was assessed at 11,000 asses. The rest of the population whose property fell below 11,000 were formed into one century and were exempt from military service.

After thus regulating the equipment and distribution of the infantry, he rearranged the cavalry. He enrolled from amongst the principal men of the state twelve centuries. In the same way he made six other centries (though only three had been formed by Romulus) under the same names under which the first had been inaugurated. For the purchase of the horse, 10,000 asses were assigned them from the public treasury; for its keep certain widows were each assessed to pay 2,000 asses annually.

The burden of all these expenses was shifted from the poor on to the rich. Then additional privileges were conferred. The former kings had maintained the constitution as handed down by Romulus, based on male suffrage in which all alike possessed the same weight and enjoyed the same rights. Servius introduced a graduation so that while no one was ostensibly deprived of his vote, all the voting power was in the hands of the principal men of the state. The knights were first summoned to record their vote, then the eighty centuries of the infantry of the First Class; if their votes were divided, which seldom happened, it was arranged for the Second Class to be summoned; very seldom did it happen that the voting extended to the lowest class.

In this 'Servian reform' the military and political roles of the Roman citizen reflected one and the same grading, determined by his position in a hierarchy based on the *census*. We should be wary of seeing in the system merely a desire to adapt the military exigencies of the state to the financial resources of the individual citizens. Such mundane preoccupations obviously did exist, for nobody could fail to see that the manning of a trireme, the upkeep of a horse or the cost of a hoplite panoply were not within every man's means. But such considerations did not become predominant until a relatively late date when people began to jib at serving the community, and to accept as an obligation what had once been sought after as a privilege, and therefore to distinguish the two sides, negative and positive, of what had originally been a single function.

Military and Social Values

In order to show more clearly the inadequacy of a purely utilitarian interpretation of this rule of proportion between the military and political functions, we must pursue the analysis in a related area, that of the qualitative (aside from the quantitative) bases for citizenship.

Citizenship had its foundation in privileges, in the land and the family, the guarantees of both social cohesion and the relations between the gods and men. And it was upon precisely these civic bases that the soldier's qualifications also rested. The good soldier was the landed proprietor. Not only is this a kind of wealth which cannot be kept hidden from the greed of the enemy in the event of defeat as can movable goods, but work on the land is a school of virtue for the citizen, as Xenophon argued in his *Oikonomikos*. From it he acquires the qualities

89

of vigilance, strength and justice which constitute the basis of military excellence. On this point, the semantic evolution of the word *ponos* (toil) is illuminating. In Homer *ponos* is military, in Hesiod agricultural, while for Xenophon it evokes a combination of energy and of endurance, in the face of pain or of effort. Hence, in classical Greece, the man of *ponos* went hunting, went to war or cultivated his land, in contrast to the craftsman who was unacquainted with *ponos* since he worked at home, like a woman. Between the two 'natural' activities, war and agriculture, strong links were forged by the political structure.

The good soldier was also the head of a family. This was not only because the desire to preserve the liberty of his children could give him added incentive for fighting, but also because, by thus realising his function as citizen, he achieved the highest degree of responsibility, to men and gods alike, which pre-disposed him to sacrifice himself for the survival of the community.*

These two theoretical bases of military excellence, inspired by the social morality, can still be seen in practice in classical Greece: on the institutional level, they were taken into consideration in Periclean Athens, in the election of *strategoi*; as an example under particular circumstances, there was the Spartan decision to recruit the elite troops sent to Thermopylae in 480 BC from the heads of families. Similarly, when the Romans had to muster freedmen, they preferred those who were landowners and heads of families. And as late as the first century AD, Onasander could still write, concerning the choice of a general (I, 12):

> I would prefer him to have children, but would not rule out a man who had none, on this account, provided he be a man of substance. If, in effect, it happens that his children are of tender years, these act as powerful philtres conveying courage which can guarantee a general's dedication to his country. They are terrible and piercing spurs capable of arousing his paternal anger against the enemy. On the other hand, if the children are fully grown, they

* Contrast the family situation of the Roman soldier in the early Empire; below, p. 115.

90

can serve him as advisers, as seconds-in-command and as confidential servants in secret matters, so that they help him to direct the affairs of the state wisely.

So we can see that both in letter and in spirit there is truth in the principle according to which warfare, at this stage of historical evolution, must have been simply 'the manifestation of a virtue natural to the citizen'.

The Political Vocation of the Soldier

Our initial proposition—a citizen is by definition a soldier,* must now be considered in the reverse formulation—a soldier tends by definition to behave as a citizen. A number of marginal cases, in particular, pinpoint the natural transition from military to political qualification.

This interchange of civic values presumably operated without difficulty at the beginning of Roman history, when the army was actually called the *populus*. In the Greek world it made itself felt much longer because there political life was moulded in a legal and institutional framework that was less constricting than the Roman. It even took on particular importance from the end of the fifth century BC, when the complexity of military operations and political crisis tended, in fact, if not in law, to increase the citizen-soldier's autonomy of action. A Greek army isolated in enemy territory could dream of setting itself up as a city, as the Athenians did at the end of the Sicilian expedition. Conversely, a city stripped of its non-combatants felt it right to try to survive in the form of a permanent army, as was envisaged by a future king of Sparta, Archidamus (360–338) according to the sixth oration of Isocrates. Now this double-beat systolic and diastolic of a city occasionally contracting into an army, of an army expanding into a city, is to be accounted for by the original identity, still clearly perceived, of the soldier and the citizen. And the same archaic feature was still to be found in the Hellenistic period in certain national monarchies, Macedon for instance, where the army assembly played the deliberative role, in certain contexts, of the assembly of citizens in the classical Greek cities.

* Even in the Hellenistic period, as we shall see, the citizen was still attached at least to the external forms of the warrior function.

The increased use of mercenaries in the Greek world from the fourth century BC of course had the effect, as we shall see, of separating political from military power. Even so, the soldiers still wished to set themselves up as a political power, just as the citizens remained attached to certain appearances of a military life. Xenophon seems to have anticipated this development when he employed the army and the general as models of political organisation and power. In the *Anabasis*, the military camp was the most perfect, because the most rational, image of the city; later, in the *Cyropaedia*, on the same principle, inspired by his own military experience, he constructed the ideal kingdom of Cyrus the Great. In fact, the Ten Thousand of the *Anabasis* played the role of a civic community on several occasions, and in the *Siegecraft* of Aeneas the Tactician we find an army treating on an equal footing with an organised state and sending it ambassadors.

Even in the Hellenistic kingdoms, where in normal times real political power was wholly beyond their reach, the professional soldiers tried to retain a 'political' activity comparable in formal terms with that of the citizens (itself more often than not reduced to very little). They regrouped themselves into associations (*politeumata, koina*) the characteristics of which varied widely: some were founded on age (*ephebes*, youths, veterans), others on membership in the same army corps, on participation in the same campaign, on being stationed in a particular place or region, on the real or imagined identity of their land of origin (ethnic, or pseudo-ethnic associations), on equality of rank or similarity of duties, increasingly on a cult or on a cultural centre, usually a gymnasium. All these groups were set up on Greek models and as such possessed an embryonic political life, scaled down in keeping with the Hellenistic situation, with some sort of constitution (*politeia*), granted or at least recognised by the sovereign, deliberative assemblies, limited elections, the right to vote on honorary decrees and sometimes a certain financial autonomy. They thus presented the image of a city without a territory, without an urban complex, and without any real independence, but at least they assured their members some semblance of political life. A certain *esprit-de-corps* therefore grew up among them, which sometimes manifested itself in a spectacular fashion in revolts, even though it was never directed in a stable or lasting way against their employers. The state founded by mercenaries from Campania, the Mamertines, on the coasts of the Straits of Messina, in about 280, was in effect based upon national rather than professional solidarity.

Even when an army established itself on the periphery of the civic body, it tended to assume the same functions as the latter, and to mould itself in the same institutional framework.

GREEK MERCENARIES

So long as the city managed to control the interplay of social and economic forces internally and to limit the field and scope of its military activities externally, it was able to preserve the original equivalence of the political and military functions and thus to ensure the theoretical homogeneity of the civic body. This was the fundamental condition for its survival, the nerve centre of its organisation. The proof is that the crisis of the city-state first made itself felt at this point; in Greece brutally, in the form of the rise of the mercenary armies; among the Romans more insidiously, in the gangrenous growth of military professionalism.

The mercenary is a professional soldier whose behaviour is determined not by his membership in a political community but by the lure of profit. The combination of three characteristics— being a specialist, an expatriate and a wage-earner—was pecu- liar to this type of man in the ancient world as in the modern. Ancient armies were rarely without some mercenaries, partly because every society includes a percentage of brawlers and adventurers naturally attracted to this profession, but above all because that was a way to fill certain branches of the army requiring a long period of training. Thus the Greeks had always preferred to recruit their archers from Crete, failing that from Persia or Scythia; the Roman archers, in the Empire, often came from Numidia or Arabia. As for slingers, they came especially from the Balearic Islands, famed beyond all other regions such as Rhodes, Acarnania, Achaea, Sicily, Spain or North Africa. And we should mention the Spartan generals, always the most prized on the Mediterranean market.

During the archaic period, the actual number of mercenaries operating in Greece proper appears to have been relatively small, a few hundred or so in the personal bodyguards of certain tyrants. Many more Greeks were then serving in oriental armies, especially in Egypt where during the seventh and sixth centuries they were the basis of the military power of the Saite dynasty. There were rather fewer in Mesopotamia, whence Antimenides, the brother of the poet Alcaeus, returned with a sword with an ivory pommel and golden trimmings as a reward for his services, or in Lydia where they were attracted by the fabled wealth of the Mermnad dynasty. Archaeological traces still survive: graffiti on the legs of the colossi at Abu-Simbel in Nubia, an encampment at Tell Defenneh on the edge of the Nile Delta, fragments of their pottery in the Negev fortresses, and so on.

This large-scale employment of Greek mercenaries reflects the recognition by eastern monarchs of the technical superiority of the hoplite armament and formation. More than that, it marks the emergence of the 'mercenary system', which implies that the mercenaries had become sufficiently numerous to have an appreciable, and sometimes determining, influence on the military life and, more widely, on the life of a society in general. Its appearance reveals a social pathology, no longer merely an individual one.

From the Greek point of view, however, their mercenaries in the east were just another aspect of the vast migration of the first half of the first millennium which was responsible for the diffusion of Hellenism all along the coasts of the Mediterranean. Then, from about 525, when the colonisation impetus had dwindled, there is hardly any mention of Greek mercenaries in the eastern Mediterranean for about a century. For a time Sicily was an exception because tyrannies lasted longer there, under the Carthaginian threat, and later the Persian satrapies of Asia Minor were another exception.

The Peloponnesian War saw the resurgence of the mercenary system, and this time it continued until the end of the Hellenistic period. For the years 401 and 400 Xenophon's *Anabasis* brings us into the presence of more than 10,000 Greek mercenaries in the service of Cyrus, the pretender to the Persian throne. Was this a sequel to the long conflict which had torn the Greek world apart? No doubt, but there was more to it. The mercenary system began to stand out distinctly at precisely this point, and to expand: some 20,000 mercenaries were operating in the eastern Mediterranean in the middle of the fourth century, half of them inside Greece; in 329 there were 50,000 in Alexander's armies. Eventually they constituted, in one form or another, the main core of the armed forces in the Hellenistic armies, so much so that the words for mercenary (*misthophoros*), foreigner (*xenos*), and soldier (*stratiotes*) began to be assimilated into each other.

With the increase in both supply and demand, the recruitment of mercenaries tended to become organised and systematised. The states did their best to ensure this, either by concluding among themselves agreements giving them exclusive rights or the first choice, by taking into their service the leaders of mercenary bands, or by sending emissaries to the 'markets' such as Cape Taenarum on the south coast of the Peloponnese where out-of-work soldiers congregated. Little by little, certain main routes of military migration began to emerge. In the Ptolemaic armies of the third century BC, for example, at a time when Egypt was asserting her supremacy in the Aegean, there was extensive recruitment from the Aegean islands and from Anatolia. However, these movements were subject to many fluctuations. Some were short-lived, the result of fortuitous changes in the demand for soldiers; some lasted longer, as the available manpower gradually became depleted. The latter reason explains the rapid drop in the Hellenisation of mercenaries in the course of the third century: a lack of Greeks and Macedonians, who had been in demand for too long, made it necessary to fall back on semi-barbarian peoples from the Balkans and Asia (apart from the Cretans and Spartans whose military reputation was well established).

The Problem of Pay

In ancient armies pay was not the only remuneration for the soldier: he could always hope to receive a share of the booty. Although the citizen-soldiers also received pay (in Greece from the beginning of the fifth century BC, and in Rome, it was said, from the time of the siege of Veii), peculiarly delicate problems arose with the mercenaries in as much as the pay was, in their eyes, the prime justification for the risks they ran. In general, pay took various forms, a sum in cash (*opsonion, misthos*), rations of corn or other foodstuffs (*sitos, metrema*), part or all

95

of which could be converted into cash, subsidiary payments for the upkeep of horses, for clothing or equipment (usually optional), the right to revictual at cut prices in the markets (*agorai*), established specially for them, and all sorts of exceptional rewards.

Along with the conditions of service, pay was a permanent source of difficulty between employees and employers. The former were constantly pressing to maintain and increase their gains, while the latter were invariably unwilling and often unable to produce the back pay due at the end of a campaign. This fundamental conflict of interests sometimes degenerated into open revolts which periodically undermined the authority of the monarchs or brought about the downfall of a city which had erred through improvidence. After the First Punic War, for example, a rebellion brought Carthage to the very brink of ruin.

As a general rule, however, efforts were made to forestall such rebellions before they got out of hand, by drawing up formal agreements like those between foreign powers. Here, for example, are a few of the stipulations in the agreement concluded in about 260 BC between Eumenes I of Pergamum and his rebellious mercenaries:*

> Demands granted by Eumenes son of Philetaerus to the soldiers of Philetaera and Attaleia: wheat to be paid for at the rate of four drachmas per medimnus; wine at four drachmas per metretes; the year of service to be fixed at ten months and no intercalary month shall be introduced; those who have served their time and find themselves unemployed, to receive the same pay as during their service; the care of orphans to fall to the nearest relative or to the person designated by the deceased; the dispensation from tax obligations granted in the regnal year 44 to be maintained. . . .

Then come the oaths exchanged by the two parties:

> I swear by Zeus, the Earth, the Sun, Poseidon, Demeter, Ares, Athena Areia, the Tauropolos and all the other gods and goddesses. To the best of my ability I shall be recon-

Die Staatsverträge des Altertums, Vol. III (1969) ed. H. H. Schmitt, no. 481.

96

ciled with Eumenes, son of Philetaerus. I shall prove my loyalty to him and his family and I shall not form any plot against Eumenes son of Philetaerus, nor shall I bear arms against him, nor shall I abandon Eumenes but shall fight for him and his in life and unto death. I shall also serve him in other ways loyally and honestly, with all my zeal and to the utmost of my strength. If I learn of any plot against Eumenes son of Philetaerus or of any enterprise harmful to his person or to his interests, I shall oppose it to the utmost of my strength and I shall immediately, or as soon as I possibly can, denounce to Eumenes son of Philetaerus, or to anyone whom I judge able to report to him at the earliest opportunity, the man who would commit such an action. If I receive from him a city or a fort or ships or goods or anything else he might commit to me, I shall defend them and hand them back in all justice and fairness to Eumenes son of Philetaerus, or to the man he has charged to receive them as soon as he, for his part, has executed the agreements. I shall not receive any letter or any envoy sent from his adversaries, and I shall never send any to them. . . . Nor shall I allow myself to be involved in any treacherous machination against this oath, by any artifice or on any pretext. . . . If I remain loyal to my oath and faithful to Eumenes son of Philetaerus, may all go well for me and mine; if I violate my oath and transgress against any of the agreements, may I perish and my posterity with me.

Eumenes' oath is as follows :

I swear by Zeus, the Earth, the Sun, Poseidon, Apollo, Demeter, Ares, Athena Areia, the Tauropolos, and all the other gods and goddesses I shall prove my loyalty to Paramonos, to the captains and all the other mercenaries in the army of Philetaera-under-Ida under the command of Paramonos; to Arces and the garrison troops under his orders; to Philonides and the non-mercenary soldiers who joined in the oath, to them and all their men; to Polylaus, the captains and all the rest of the soldiers under his command at Attaleia, infantrymen, cavalry and Trallians* so

* A Thracian people.

long as they serve with us. I shall not form any plot and no one else will do so in my name. I shall not deliver up to any adversary either their persons or anything that might belong to them, nor their leaders, nor the elected representatives of their association, neither by any machination nor upon any pretext. I shall not bear arms against them. . . .

There could be no better documentation of the power relations underlying the fragile agreements for collaboration between mercenaries and their employers.

The Cleruchs

It is then understandable that employers should have tried to ensure the loyalty of their troops by other means. Cities did this by awarding honours and sometimes even citizenship. Kings did it essentially by grants of land, which had the twofold advantage of attaching the mercenaries and their dependents to the service of a dynasty, and of settling the delicate problem of pay in the cheapest way, given the weak development of a monetary economy in certain eastern monarchies.

Military colonisation took different forms according to the natural resources of the various kingdoms and the political ambitions of their sovereigns. In the Seleucid and Attalid monarchies it was effected by new foundations, rural or urban, with or without the status of a city. From a military point of view they were permanent units of self-defence who also contributed their quota to the royal forces when necessary. By thus strengthening the political structure of the empire, the sovereigns at the same time facilitated the settlement and integration of the immigrants by providing them with new living conditions similar to those they had relinquished at home.

But this system was unacceptable to the Ptolemies who tried to ensure their rule in Egypt in a very different way, without disrupting the internal coherence and unity of an indigenous society whose submissiveness seemed splendidly guaranteed by the weight of the institutions inherited from a distant and glorious Egyptian past. In keeping with these traditions, the Ptolemies preferred a type of individual rural settlement where each soldier (*cleruch*) was directly responsible to the king for his plot of land (*kleros*). These plots varied in size according to the nationality, rank and branch of service of each soldier. They were between 5 and 20 arourai (one aroura was just over two-thirds of an acre) for a native soldier (*machimos*), and between 20 and 100 arourai for a Greek mercenary whose leaders might receive any amount up to 10,000 arourai. Although they could be situated anywhere in the valley of the Nile, the maximum concentration was in middle Egypt and around Lake Moeris at the apex of the delta as part of a programme to reclaim desert and marshland.

The Ptolemaic *cleruch* was a peasant-soldier and his essential duties were to farm his land and hold himself in readiness for a call-up from the sovereign. He was also subject to taxes, both those which fell on every land-owner in Egypt and those which followed from his particular status of cleruch (such as taxes for the equipment of triremes, for the payment of secretaries, doctors and veterinary surgeons). In compensation, he received pay from the State as well as rewards and booty during military operations.

The details underwent changes in the course of the Hellenistic period. Under Ptolemy I Soter, who inaugurated the system, and Ptolemy II Philadelphus, who developed it, the cleruch in effect had only the use of his land. The King remained the owner, and on the death of the *cleruch* or in the event of his failing to fulfil his duties, the allotment returned to the crown. Hence the holder could not dispose of the land at will; he could neither bequeath it nor sell it, though from the start he had the right to let it. Subsequently a natural evolution, already detectable at the end of the third century BC, transformed this precarious possession, personal and revocable, into an hereditary property, and then into one which could be transferred outside the family provided that the new holder assumed the military and fiscal obligations of his predecessor. Similarly the dwelling (*stathmos*) allotted to the cleruch in a native village near his holding underwent an even more rapid transformation and became private property. Whether they liked it or not, the Ptolemies were forced to accept the new state of affairs. It was, anyway, to their advantage, as the decrease in immigrants from the end of the third century BC compelled them to depend more and more on the descendants of cleruchs for their armed forces.

The Mercenaries in Hellenistic Society

The mercenaries left a deep mark on Hellenistic society, in the first place through their direct intervention in political life at the instigation of their employers. They supported the recrudescent tyrannies in Greece and on the borders of the large empires, and in the latter they maintained the power of the kings. Whether concentrated in urban citadels, posted along the frontiers or spread through the countryside, they were alternately, and sometimes simultaneously, protectors and oppressors. It was they who conferred power, glory and wealth, they who were neither citizens nor subjects but simply instruments of domination, foreign to the political game (unless, as we have seen, they were clandestinely involved).

Even more lasting was their cultural influence in the eastern regions which Alexander's conquests had opened to Greek civilisation. These expatriates sought to recreate around them the type of life to which they were accustomed. Their starting point was usually the gymnasium, a centre for physical training, recreation and study, and their cultural activity was essentially religious in form. They kept up their old national and local cults and they worshipped various 'saviour' gods (more than typically 'professional' deities such as the Macedonian Tauropolos). The intensity of this effort at preserving Greek culture varied in time and place: it increased in the second century BC precisely when there were fewer Greeks among the new recruits, and the most spectacular manifestations appeared on the borders of the eastern empires, where the threat of isolation among an often hostile indigenous population was greatest.

There is little uncontaminated documentation for the psychology of the mercenaries: a few funeral monuments from Sidon in Phoenicia and Demetrias in Thessaly, the odd epigram or popular song, some meagre private archives from Egypt. Without the official texts, therefore, that bear witness to their political activities and their cultural preoccupations, it would be impossible to mitigate the discredit cast upon them by contemporary writers, most of whom were from aristocratic families. Isocrates had set the tone as early as the first half of the fourth century; he was tireless in stigmatising the 'brigandage, the violence and the injustices of those people, the common enemies of the whole human race.' (VIII, 45–6).

Then came the writers of Middle and New Comedy and their Roman imitators. We are all familiar with Pyrogopolinices ('Conqueror-of-fortified-places') in the *Miles Gloriosus* of Plautus, a braggart, a dungheap, a load of perjury and adultery; or Thraso the 'Bold', in Terence's *The Eunuch*, the captain bamboozled by the courtesan Thais who saw nothing in him but foolishness and bragging. The same comic figure of the mercenary appears in a fresco at Pompeii, leaning proudly on his lance, while he listens with a hard and obtuse expression to the flatteries of his sycophant. The picture is too exaggerated not to be unjust, though we should not rush to gild it out of philhellenism. The Greek mercenary was presumably no better and no worse than the hardened trooper of any age.

The Causes of the Mercenary System

Before it became an essential factor in the evolution of Greek society, the mercenary system was a product of that society, not merely a response to the demands of military technique.

Even if a time did come when military technique required a shift to professionalism, the citizens could have become professionals, as they did in the Roman Empire. But they refused, because that would have meant a renunciation of their essentially political calling and therefore a mortal blow to the city-state system. This incompatibility between the political function and the military function became even sharper in the Hellenistic period, when the centres where the soldiers signed on did not coincide with the areas where they were recruited.

In short, it was not demand that created the supply, nor function that created the instrument. At the most, demand gave an orientation to certain social, or rather asocial, types who were already so predisposed. This is shown, in the first place, by the fact that the mercenary system appeared in Greece in the archaic period and again in the fourth century BC along with colonisation and tyranny, two other major symptoms of social crisis. The first two function as safety valves; if one becomes blocked the other plays a fuller role, as in the fourth century when Isocrates both denounced 'the running sore of the mercenary system' and indicated the cure, a revival of colonial expansion, this time in Asia. As for tyranny, in the last resort it brought to the surface on the political level the insoluble contradictions within the city-state.

A second argument is provided by the geographical origins of the mercenaries. The first to appear, at the beginning of the Peloponnesian War, in the western satrapies of the Persian kingdom more than in Greece itself, were Arcadians and Achaeans who later made up the majority of the companions-in-arms of Xenophon in Asia (about 6,000 out of 10,400 men). It is impossible to see these figures as a coincidence arising out of the war, since the war did not touch the centre of the Peloponnese. Similarly, in the Hellenistic period, central and northern Greece and Anatolia, which had suffered little in the conflicts of the fourth century, replaced the Peloponnese as the main source of mercenaries. Although it is difficult in each of these instances to determine the relative importance of demographic pressures, social unrest, economic difficulties, political accidents and foreign appeals, the regularity of the phenomenon is convincing evidence of the depth of the crisis which had produced it.

A final argument stems from the glimpse available to us of the standard of living of these mercenaries, based solely on their pay without considering food allowances or unexpected income from booty or from the occasional generosity of an employer. The soldiers in the Peloponnesian War all appear to have received more or less the same pay, whether they served as citizens, allies or mercenaries: one drachma a day at the beginning of the war and just over half a drachma at the end. Cyrus, at the beginning of his campaign, promised his troops one daric or one Cyricene stater a month, roughly 25 Athenian drachmas. During the Hellenistic period the tariff (apparently the same for allies as for mercenaries) appears to have been slightly more than one Athenian drachma. These sums hardly amounted to more than the pay of a manual worker with average skill. In normal times, therefore, there was little need to increase the pay in order to encourage applicants. It was the pressure of supply, rather than of demand, which swelled the ranks of the mercenary armies.

A passage in Xenophon's *Anabasis* (VI, 4, 8) is sometimes quoted against this conclusion. He writes:

> For most of the soldiers had sailed away from Greece to undertake this service for pay, not because their means were scanty, but because they knew by report of the noble character of Cyrus; some brought other men with them, some had even spent money of their own on the enterprise . . .

However, apart from the fact that this remark can apply only to a minority who had come especially from Greece, the key seems to lie in the author's desire to raise the social standing of those who were to become his own subordinates.

In sum, the Greek mercenary system was not dissociated from social and political disintegration. On the contrary it grew out of the crisis accompanying the birth, and later death, of the city-state, with its inflexible framework unable to withstand the pressure of internal antagonisms. On the other hand, in certain periods, especially among the peripheral, less highly structured barbarian communities, the relationships of supply and demand were reversed, and then the upward surge of the mercenary system accelerated as it gathered momentum, and helped aggravate the social crisis which created it.

ROMAN PROFESSIONALISM

The Decline of the Citizen-Soldier

The Hellenistic mercenary system made little progress in the Roman world when, some two centuries later, it was confronted with the same problem of recruitment. The Romans turned to mercenaries only for certain kinds of specialists, for instance, Cretan archers or slingers from the Balearic Islands. Roman imperialism, based on the voluntary or forced cooperation of the conquered peoples, accompanied by the spread of citizenship, a privileged status with a rapidly disappearing political function, gave birth to a professional army composed as much of citizens as of aliens (*peregrini*) who were subject to Rome and who found the army a path to citizenship.

This development was launched in the second century

103

BC by a crisis in the traditional system of military recruitment which was itself but one aspect of a larger social crisis provoked by the increasing frequency and scale of military operations.

The proprietors of small or medium-sized holdings, who provided the greater part of the citizen armies, were injured directly. They were the first to suffer from the ravages inflicted upon Italy by Hannibal and his allies during the second Punic War. Livy writes (XXVIII, 11, 8):

> The smallholders had been carried off by the war, there was hardly any servile labour available, the cattle had been driven off as plunder, and the homesteads had been either stripped or burnt.

And it was they, too, who were most affected by longer campaigns farther afield, as Rome extended its empire in the Mediterranean area. Kept from home by their military duties often for years at a time, particularly in Spain, they were unable to look after their farms. Forced into debt or obliged to sell their land, they lost the regular income which was the qualification for recruitment.

But this worsening of the condition of the peasants with small or average holdings also appears, in other respects, to be an indirect consequence of the wars. For while the soldier-citizens were growing poorer, the senatorial aristocracy and, to a much smaller extent, the urban plebs were reaping the benefits of Roman imperialism.

The aristocracy secured most of the gains of war, in fact if not in law, in particular the *ager Romanus* which was steadily expanding through confiscations of conquered territory. Originally enjoying a simple right of occupation in these vast domains, wealthy Romans, Appian explains (*Civil Wars* 1, 7),

> were getting possession of the greater part of the undistributed lands. Emboldened by the lapse of time to believe that they would never be dispossessed, absorbing any adjacent strips and their poor neighbours' allotments, partly by purchase under persuasion and partly by force, they came to cultivate vast tracts instead of single estates, using slaves as labourers and herdsmen, lest free labourers should

be drawn from agriculture into the army. At the same time the ownership of slaves brought them great gain from the multitude of their progeny, who increased because they were exempt from military service. Thus certain powerful men became extremely rich and the race of slaves multiplied throughout the country, while the Italian people dwindled in numbers and strength, being oppressed by penury, taxes and military service. If they had any respite from these evils they passed their time in idleness, because the land was held by the rich, who employed slaves instead of free men as cultivators.

Booty and tribute flooded into Rome from the provinces while the tax farmers (*publicani*) and Italian merchants moved in the wake of the armies, and with their protection. Inevitably the Roman economy suffered an upheaval from this influx of wealth, cheaply acquired through conquest or through commerce. The effects were felt in the monetary sector, disturbing the census system, and even more in agriculture. The massive imports of wheat from overseas seriously competed with cereal production of Italy, stimulating a shift to vines and olive trees and to herding, a conversion in which only the more wealthy could succeed.

The peasants, without hope of improving their situation by remaining on the land, flocked into the city of Rome. Sometimes they found work there, particularly in the building projects undertaken by the state and by the aristocracy. But it was more attractive to cash in on their political rights, and thus to collect a few crumbs from the victors' table. It was in the second century B C that the increase in free distributions (*largitiones*) on the part of the great families, concerned to ensure success in the elections, cultivated in the Roman habits of political clientship. The Roman plebs were both susceptible to the attractions of city life and concerned to find a favourable position from which to use and abuse official and private largesse. Hence they were unreliable supporters of such reformers as the Gracchi who sought to reestablish a sound basis for Rome's military expansion by restoring a thriving peasant class in Italy. Instead, the easy way out, the proletarianisation of the army, short-sightedly favoured by the Senate, won the day.

The Proletarianisation of the Army

When Polybius was writing in the middle of the second century BC, the minimum qualification for the fifth class had already fallen from 11,000 to 4,000 asses, and it soon dropped to 1,500. At the same time frequent calls for volunteers, in preference to conscripts, increased the opportunities for the proletariat to enter the legions. When Marius decided in 107 to recruit his soldiers 'not according to the classes in the manner of our forefathers, but allowing anyone to volunteer, for the most part the proletariat' (Sallust, *Jugurtha,* 86), he was simply carrying earlier developments to their logical conclusion and sanctioning what was to a large extent already a state of fact. The Marian 'reform' was further extended by the Social War of 91–89 BC, when a number of freedmen, if not outright aliens, were introduced into the legions. And after citizenship was extended to the whole of Italy in 88, it was easy to meet army needs largely by appealing for volunteers.

Under the early Empire military service continued to be theoretically compulsory for all citizens.* There were in fact times, especially in the early years, when conscription was resorted to, although there was always the possibility of evasion by procuring a substitute. However the volunteers usually sufficed to fill the gaps in the army, given that only about one twentieth of each age-class was required, except on the rare occasions when entirely new legions were created. The imperial recruiting officers (*dilectatores*) had to do little more than make sure that the candidate was a citizen (or that it was possible to grant him citizenship), that he was honest, and of course that his physical qualities were satisfactory, the ideal height was 1·72m (5 feet 10 inches) and the preferred age 18–23. Good letters of reference obviously improved the candidate's chances.

Most of the recruits were men of modest means, often from a rural background. The urban plebs were increasingly inclined to sit at home, picking up without effort the benefits of imperialism in the shape of gratuities (*sportulae*), while the provincial bourgeoisie were kept busy by their commercial activities, their

---

* Citizenship, which might be granted at the time of enrolment, remained a necessary qualification for a legionary.

political ambitions and their taste for luxury. Under these conditions there was no alternative but to fall back upon the peasantry who, in Italy, were continuing to suffer from a serious economic crisis, and who in the rest of the Empire were also paying the price for the increase in urbanisation.

Even at the end of the fourth century AD Vegetius (I, 3) was writing:

> I do not believe that there has ever been any doubt that the rural plebs are the most suitable for the military profession. These people thrive on fresh air and hard work, enduring the heat of the sun, not seeking the shade, knowing nothing of baths, unaccustomed to sensual pleasures, simple of soul, contented with little, their limbs hardened by all kinds of labour so that they easily acquire the habit of forging iron, digging trenches and carrying heavy burdens.

There was, however, reason to fear the political and military consequences of too great a proletarianisation of the army. Hence the efforts of certain emperors, such as Augustus, to raise the social level of the recruits. They did this either by conscription which brought into the legions a number of individuals from the middle strata; or else, in a more systematic way, by extending the catchment area to those provinces which were in the process of Romanisation, where the army continued to be regarded, for a certain period, as an essential means to social promotion.

The Provincialisation of the Legions

Until the time of Augustus rural recruits were Italians for the most part. Later, the Italians (still preferred in the praetorian cohorts) were progressively supplanted in the legions by men from the provinces. Under Trajan, it has been estimated that the Italians were outnumbered by four or five to one. By the end of the second century, Hyginus could define the legionary forces as a *militia provincialis fidelissima.* Italians were now called upon to serve only in exceptional circumstances. At first, the provincials came from the regions that had been conquered earliest, the Narbonne area, Spain, Africa and Macedonia; then, as Romanisation spread, they were joined by the long-haired

Gauls and men from Noricum on the upper Danube, Syria, Palestine, Numidia, then from Germany, Pannonia, Moesia along the middle and lower reaches of the Danube, Thrace and Epirus. All of these went to make up legions which can be divided by their language into Graeco–Oriental and Latin–Occidental. Yet another step was taken in the second and third centuries AD, when it became customary to recruit even more locally, in the immediate neighbourhood of a garrison town and often among the children of legionaries (the *ex castris*).

A number of factors should be borne in mind, over and above the social problems already mentioned. Southern Italy had declined in population, and Italians had anyway enjoyed the privilege of serving in the praetorian and urban cohorts until the reign of Septimius Severus. The demographic situation of the individual provinces and their varying contributions of auxiliary troops constituted another factor. Finally, there was the military policy of those emperors who felt the need of tying troops more closely to the regions they were assigned to defend, in order to raise morale and improve their fighting power and efficiency.

Conscription in the Late Empire

The edict of Caracalla, in 212, which extended citizenship to most of the free men in the Empire, must have swelled the sources of recruitment considerably. However, the anarchy of the third century soon made it impossible to rely on volunteers to meet the escalating military requirements (except at times in a few provinces, such as Illyricum). It became necessary, from the time of Diocletian, who also doubled the number of soldiers, to adopt a more regular and more authoritarian form of enrolment.

Diocletian introduced a twofold reform. On the one hand he gave official approval to admission into the army of children born in the camps (*ex castris*); on the other hand, he imposed upon the rest of the population, with rare exceptions, the duty of providing recruits in proportion to the fiscal charges on individuals (*capitatio*) and on the land (*iugatio*). In each city, certain large landowners, known as *capitularii* or *temonarii*, were charged with seeing to it that the fiscal unit to which they belonged provided either a specified number of recruits or the money (*aurum tironicum*) for the maintenance of substitutes. In theory the state was thus in a position to regulate and direct recruitment according to its needs and to the military aptitude of the various peoples concerned. In fact, the reform quickly misfired on account of the heavy demand for substitutes and the poor quality of the recruits.

Eventually the lower classes, under pressure from the *capitularii*, came to bear the full brunt of the military burden, while the recruiters were diverting a considerable share of the *aurum tironicum* into their own pockets. The military profession still remained more or less respected, according to region. It found more acceptance in the frontier provinces (Gaul, Illyricum or Thrace, for example), where military service was traditional, than in the provinces of the interior where such a tradition was unknown and where the threat of conscription was frequently enough to prompt men to flee to some distant land. As a result, the recruits were generally poor quality and in morale, chosen as they were from the lowest strata of the rural population, tramps, idlers and freed slaves. Not surprisingly, although the principles laid down by Diocletian remained unchanged throughout the fourth century, many emperors attempted to correct some of the weaknesses. In 375, Valens tried to equalise the burdens and define the responsibilities. Other emperors fixed heavy penalties for attempts to evade conscription by cutting off a thumb. Recruits were tattooed as a check against desertion. Yet declining quality had to be faced and in 367 the minimum height for a conscript was lowered from 5 feet 10 inches to 5 feet 7 inches (Roman),* at a time when the army had long been open to barbarians.

Aliens and Barbarians

After the Social War, the Italian allies were called upon to serve in the legions. To replace them Rome recruited an increasing number of alien auxiliaries in the provinces. Their status remained uncertain to the end of the Republic but was fixed at the beginning of the Empire, by which time they made up about half the army.

---

* The Roman foot was 296 mm.

Recruiting policy was originally determined by local needs, then organised according to the needs of the Empire in general and the military qualifications of the subject peoples. The trend was to rely more and more on the less Romanised provinces, while the recruits, obliged to serve far from their native provinces, gradually found that their units had lost their national characteristics. Eventually Trajan felt the need to restore the original flexibility of the system. He created new auxiliary units, by allied peoples, the so-called *numeri* of infantrymen and the *cunei* of cavalry, and an attempt was made to preserve their ethnic homogeneity.

Thus, from the beginning of the Empire, Rome extended the area from which it recruited its defenders even beyond the limits of the provinces. This tendency was considerably accelerated in the third century, and the principal characteristic of armed forces of the Late Empire was the increasing participation of barbarians, first and foremost Germans. Some, 'federated' tribes living on the borders of or even within the Empire, provided contingents who fought for Rome under the command of their own national chieftains. Others were integrated in the Roman army either individually or in groups, as prisoners of war, as volunteers (especially if they came from outside the Empire) —or in fulfilment of the *deditio* agreement which gave them the right to settle in the provinces. These barbarian recruits are hardly distinguishable from the so-called *laeti* (particularly numerous in Gaul and in the Po valley from the end of the third century), former citizens or allies who had fallen into the hands of barbarians and were then returned to provincial territory.

These soldiers, whose 'Romanness' was questionable, to say the least, sometimes formed relatively homogeneous units with names reflecting their origins, while others were brigaded with citizens. In neither case do they seem to have been more inclined to treachery than anyone else (except to some degree when they faced their own compatriots in battle). Since their traditional tribal rivalry prevented them from developing any real spirit of national solidarity which might have united them against the Romans, they had every reason to attach themselves to an Empire which made their fortune and which held great cultural attractions for them. In this connection it is significant that from the time of Augustus barbarians made up a substantial proportion of the imperial bodyguard (the *collegium Germanorum*), later the *equites singulares*, and finally in the Late Empire the *scholae palatinae*.

It is also significant that we never hear of a barbarian soldier who had to return to his native land on his retirement. Perhaps they could expect little or no good from their own kin, if we may accept an anecdote in the *History* of Ammianus Marcellinus (XI, 5, 5–16) concerning a Frankish chieftain, the master of the foot for Constantius II in 355:

> Meanwhile Silvanus, stationed at Cologne and learning from his friends' constant messages what Apodemius was undertaking to the ruin of his fortunes, knowing the pliant mind of the fickle emperor and fearing lest he should be condemned to death absent and unheard, was put in a most difficult position and thought of entrusting himself to the good faith of the savages. But he was prevented by Laniogaisus. . . . He assured Silvanus that the Franks, whose fellow-countryman he was, would kill him or on receipt of a bribe betray him. So Silvanus, seeing no safety under present conditions, was driven to extreme measures, and having gradually spoken more boldly with the chief officers, he aroused them by the greatness of the reward he promised; then as a temporary expedient he tore the purple decorations from the standards of the cohorts and the companies, and so mounted to the imperial dignity.

The non-citizens upon whom Rome tended to depend more and more for its defence were not genuine mercenaries, since in most cases they were serving Rome as a result of an agreement of mutual assistance concluded with their native communities. Usually they had no desire to return home and served always in the hope of thereby gaining some new political qualification within the framework of Roman institutions. In the end, in the fourth century, the Empire fell into the hands of barbarian generals who took the supreme power under their protection when they did not actually seize it. In 394, for instance, it was the Goths Gainas and Alaric, the Vandal Stilicho and the Caucasian Bacurius who presented Theodosius I with victory over the usurper Eugenius (his army was under the command of the Frank, Arbogast).

Roman Professionalism

Unless they were able to progress to power within the army itself, by promotion up the military hierarchy, both citizens and candidates for citizenship had to wait for their retirement before they could participate in political life, in most cases in some provincial municipality. On entering the army they had in effect signed a contract which turned them into professional soldiers for a period of years. This military professionalism became a significant factor from the beginning of the first century BC along with the proletarianisation of the legions, although it was officially sealed only by Augustus after the civil wars.

The length of military service, which still varied between five and twenty years in Caesar's time, was fixed at the beginning of the first century AD at sixteen years for the praetorian cohorts, twenty for the urban cohorts and the legions, twenty-five for the auxiliary forces, and even more for the navy (twenty-six years between Vespasian and Antoninus Pius, twenty-eight from the time of Caracalla). With increasing frequency, furthermore, legionaries continued to serve or be recalled as veterans (*evocati*), or they were not discharged until well after the expiry of the legal term, and only then by showing the utmost determination.

The increased length of military service ensured the permanence of military units, that of the legions from the time of the civil wars, that of the auxiliary forces from the reign of Augustus, and as a result they each acquired a distinctive personality. The civil war legions were given an ordinal number by whoever formed them. Augustus having thus inherited several parallel systems of numbering, added an official name (*cognomen*) when he reorganised the Roman army. The name might reflect the circumstances of a legion's formation. Legions I and II *Adiutrix* were created as a complement to the existing units; Legion X *Fretensis* came out of the navy; Legions VII, X, XII, XIV *Gemina* resulted from the fusion of two legions. Or it could take the name of the founder (Legions I *Macriana*; II, III and VIII *Augusta*; II *Traiana*; XXII *Deiotariana*; XXX *Ulpia*), of his favourite god (Legions XV *Apollinaris*; XIII and

112

XV *Primigenia*), of a dynasty (Legions I, IV, and XVI *Flavia*). Other names expressed geographical origin (Legions I, II, and III *Italica*; I, II, and III *Parthica*; III *Gallica*; V *Alaudae*, meaning 'larks' of Celtic origin); commemorated campaigns (Legions I *Germanica*, III *Cyrenaica*, IV, V, and VII *Macedonica*, IV *Scythica*, IX *Hispana*, XVI *Gallica*); or commanders (XI *Claudia*; XX *Valeria*); or reflected their reputation (Legions VI *Ferrata*, 'iron-clads', XII *Fulminata*, 'lightning', XXI *Rapax*, 'devastating'. These names were sometimes followed by propitiatory adjectives such as *Pia, Fidelis, Fortis, Concors, Firma, Constans, Victrix*. From the time of Commodus, and especially from Caracalla onwards, it became the custom to give all the legions the name of the reigning emperor, hence *Antoninianae, Severianae, Alexandrianae, Maximinianae, Gordianae, Philippianae, Gallienae,* and so on. In the same way the names of the auxiliary units indicated their national origin, composition, strength, number, the name of the provincial governor who had organised them, the locality where they were stationed, the scene of their campaigns, from Caracalla's time the name of the reigning emperor, or an honour which they had won in recognition of their services.

This personalising of the military units was carried over to veneration of their emblems, which both symbolised their permanence and their reputation and served the practical purpose of a rallying point on the field of battle. From Marius' time the eagle, the bird of Jupiter, supplanted the other old totems as the legionary emblem. By the end of the Republic it was made of silver, with a golden thunderbolt at its feet; later it was made entirely of gold or at the least of gilded silver. The famed attachment of Roman soldiers to the legionary eagles is well illustrated by the stress laid by contemporaries on winning back the eagles lost by Varus in the Teutoberg Forest. Each unit also had its own flags (*vexilla*) and insignia (*signa*), often consisting of signs of the zodiac or divine effigies, and it received a growing number of standards (*imagines*) depicting the emperor or a member of his family. All these emblems were solemnly anointed with precious oils, decorated with garlands, crowned with laurels and deposited in specially constructed chapels in the camps. And oaths were sworn before them to the great indignation of Christians such as Tertullian.

Military Pay

As soon as military professionalism joined with proletarianisation the problem of pay became acute. At the beginning of
the first century B C the financial position of the legionaries was
hardly brilliant; they still received the five asses a day, less
deductions for food and equipment, which they had drawn in
Polybius' time. Furthermore, in 141 there had been a revaluation
of the silver denarius against the bronze as, which had reduced
the silver value of a soldier's annual pay from 180 denarii to
112½. (Centurions and the cavalry remained unaffected, as their
pay was traditionally calculated in silver.) An ordinary manual
worker in Rome could now earn as much as 12 asses a day. Not
surprisingly, then, the growing impoverishment of soldiers was
a source of dissension, and Caesar doubled their pay. The new
wage, 225 denarii a year, paid in three instalments, despite
claims which sometimes led to a revolt, continued in force to
the reign of Domitian. He increased the amount by one third,
perhaps by adding a fourth annual instalment. It was probably
again increased to 450 denarii under Septimius Severus, and
to 675 under Caracalla, but this did not mean a corresponding increase in purchasing power, since silver coins had undergone a considerable devaluation.

Pay, of course, varied with rank and branch of service, in the
legions from one and a half times or double the basic pay for
non-commissioned officers, to as much as thirty times for centurions in the top class. The minimum rate in the navy was
one third of that in the legions, also in the auxiliary units where
there were great discrepancies according to the source of the
funds and the reputation of the men. Between the praetorian
cohorts and the legions the ratio in pay under the early Empire
was ten to three.

For a long time equipment costs were deducted from the pay
in order to maintain the fiction of the soldier-citizen. On the
other hand, supplementary income was available, in amounts
varying according to circumstances from booty which was
distributed according to more or less fixed rules, and from
individual looting often at the expense of the provincials themselves. Hence it was a major preoccupation of provincial cities
to obtain from the emperor a dispensation keeping armies on

manoeuvre away from their territory. The elite of the army could also count on the self-interested generosity of the masters of the Empire. In the first two centuries AD occasional gifts (*donativa*), generally equal to one third of the annual pay, were distributed to the praetorians, less frequently to the legionaries: 75 denarii in 8 BC, when his grandson entered the army, 75 at the death of Augustus, 75 at the death of Tiberius, 100 at the end of Caligula's eastern expedition, and so on. In addition there were the profitable deals that, in troubled times, were made with the candidates for the throne, like those made by Octavius and Antony after the death of Caesar with the legions stationed in Macedonia.

Each legionary deposited his savings in the bank of his cohort, and he could thus slowly accumulate a small fund (*castrense peculium*) which was handed over to him when his services came to an end. A soldier with rank could also belong to a mutual aid society (*schola*) and subscribe to the legion's funeral fund, ensuring himself a decent burial. When he left the army, unless dishonourably discharged, he was given a bonus (*praemia militiae*), normally a lump sum of 5,000 denarii for praetorians, 3,000 for legionaries. At times, however, a parcel of land was substituted on account of the impecunious state of the Empire in the first century, cheerfully accepted by the soldiers so long as it was situated in the province of their choice.

Veterans enjoyed certain fiscal privileges in some cases extended to members of their families—exemption from certain taxes and from the burdensome duties of municipal magistracies and priesthoods. There were also legal advantages, for example, retired auxiliaries were granted citizenship, until the beginning of the third century, and it was made possible for the retired legionaries, who until the time of Septimius Severus had been condemned to concubinage while in the army, to contract a legal marriage.

In the Late Empire soldiers continued to be paid a wage (*stipendium*) in cash, which was roughly equal to that which they received under the Severi, and also a number of bonuses, for example, when the emperor celebrated his birthday or his accession to the throne and when he assumed the consulate. The legionaries were assured of at least 7,500 denarii per year. No doubt Diocletian was exaggerating when he declared, in the preamble to his famous edict of maximum prices, that a single purchase was enough to exhaust the whole of this annual pay. But it is true that the real value of the sum, paid in denarii, was reduced to next to nothing from the third century by the rapid devaluation of bronze coins.

Bonuses in unminted silver or in gold coins were not enough to restore the financial position of the soldier, now ensured in the main by payments in kind, of clothing, weapons, horses and, above all, food for both men (*annona*) and animals (*capitus*). These rations, as difficult to distribute as to provide, consisted of three pounds of bread or biscuits, one litre of wine or vinegar, two pounds of fresh or salted meat, and seven centilitres of oil a day (according to Egyptian papyri), not counting the supplementary provisions issued to the sons of soldiers (until they were withdrawn late in the fourth century).

From the time of Constantine where officers were concerned, and from the end of the fourth century for the troops as a whole, it became increasingly customary for payments in kind to be converted into gold coins, according to rates which varied from place to place according to prevailing conditions. It ap-appears, furthermore, that from the fourth century, soldiers assigned to frontier duties were considered soldier–colonists, allotted parcels of land for their livelihood and therefore paid a lower salary. And when he left the army, a veteran at last received either a parcel of land (together with oxen and seedcorn), or a gift in cash if he preferred.

Against these remunerations there were a number of charges claimed more or less legally by officers and administrators. On the other hand, there were fiscal privileges, exemption from the poll-tax for troops who had served in the interior, and from the tax known as the *collatio lustralis* for veterans and their wives who set up in business.

On the whole, much as their situation varied from one province to another and even from one regiment to another, the soldiers of the Late Empire were a relatively prosperous class; all the more so if they were able to profit from the poor discipline to exercise all kinds of secondary occupations. A certain Flavius Patermuthis, for example, describes himself in a legal papyrus with quiet confidence as 'a soldier of the regiment of Elephantine, boatman by profession.'

So, at every instant in Greek and Roman history the similarity between military societies and societies in general is apparent. They are similar, not identical, for what we have here is an image, not a reflection, in that the army through a kind of 'focusing process' presents a miniature and distorted version of the social milieu from which it emerged.

The army indeed had its own traditions, founded upon the deep structures of ancient societies. It also had its own peculiar requirements often imposed by circumstances. Both could affect the particular qualifications of the individual fighting man. In order to form a more concrete idea of the groups of men under arms we must then, without going into the details of the various modes of combat, define, so to speak, their social coordinates.

THE STATUS OF FIGHTING MEN

The ancients distinguished three fundamental modes of combat: in the open, around fortifications, and on the sea. Each had its own more or less fixed level of honourability and its particular evolution of military technique. But the first type was normally the dominant one in practice and in theory, within the overall organisation of the armed forces. Not surprisingly: control of territory was the primary condition for the survival and expansion of communities and the most deeply rooted value in their ideology.

The Rise and Fall of the Cavalry

When the peoples of the Aegean area emerged from the Neolithic Age two technical innovations greatly enhanced their military potential: the use of metals, especially bronze, from the third millennium BC and the employment of the horse for traction from the beginning of the second millennium. However, these innovations did not have an impact immediately nor to the same degree everywhere. The effect on Crete, for example, was slight; at its zenith 'Minoan' Crete was a pacific society in contrast to those regions of the Greek mainland characterised from the sixteenth century by the palace civilization of the Mycenaean type. The increased power of the state made it possible to organise distant expeditions to procure the copper and tin necessary for arms, the manufacture of which

117

was entrusted to increasingly specialised craftsmen. At the same time, the breeding of horses was facilitated by the concentration of wealth in the hands of the powerful aristocracy that gravitated around the palaces.

In the late Bronze Age, then, chariots became a military essential in Greece as in the great Near-Eastern empires, more because of the quality of the combatants than of their numbers (despite reference in the Cnossus tablets to some 400 chariots and 700 horses kept in reserve by the palace). A chariot, used for hunting as for war, was normally drawn by two horses and carried a driver and an aristocratic fighting man, both protected by breast-plates.

Chariotry did not survive the collapse of the palace economies at the end of the second millennium. Homer retains the vaguest memory of it and misunderstands the tactics. In the *Iliad* the chariot is reduced to a 'taxi' for the heroes, bringing them to the scene of action, and evacuating them the moment things go wrong. Thereafter, references to chariots are rare and restricted to peripheral regions; for a time in Euboea, Boeotia, Lydia, Cyprus and Etruria; until the third century BC in Gaul; to the beginning of our era in Cyrenaica and Brittany; and in the Persian Empire in the form of the scythed chariot. The latter, first conceived by Cyrus according to Xenophon (*Cyropaedia* VI, 1), reappeared in the army of Antiochus III in 189 BC, in that of Mithridates in 86 BC and in that of his son Pharnaces II, in 47 BC, and once more in the fourth century AD, in the proposals for the military restoration of the Roman Empire projected at length by the unknown author of the *De rebus bellicia*. However, after the initial moment of surprise and panic, the ineffectiveness of the chariot is apparent and these few attempts to resurrect it were all failures.

The same is true of elephants, employed in an analogous way. Their moment of glory came at the battle of Ipsus in 301 BC, won by Seleucus I with a line of 480 beasts. Soon they, too, had to be discarded, especially in encounters with the Romans who had become accustomed to them in the Second Punic War, and after the battle of Magnesia in Asia Minor, in 189 BC, elephants were used only exceptionally. The last occasion seems to have been the battle of Thapsus in Tunisia, in 46 BC during the Roman civil wars.

Cavalry had been developed as an independent arm in Greece even before the collapse of the Mycenaean kingdoms, and it seems to have become essential in battles after the abandonment of chariots but before the creation of the hoplite formation. This dating has been challenged by historians but there is the powerful argument provided by the Campanians in Italy, who adopted the cavalry from the early Greek colonists and became specialists in that arm. And the dating is important, for indirectly it raises the question whether one can detect in the origins of the cavalry the same correlation between military, social and political functions already noted for the chariotry (and also to be found in other circumstances). Was it the case, in both Greece and in Italy, that before the consolidation of the hoplite state the aristocracy played a military role peculiar to itself and technically superior to that of the mass infantry?

Currently this question is being debated by historians particularly in connection with early Rome. One school holds that there was a close link between the primacy of the cavalry and the consolidation of a social elite (whether or not assimilated into the patrician class); the other that the hoplite infantry was the first military expression of the landed aristocracy which assumed power after the fall of the Etruscan kings. Although both views thus accept that military power was then the basis for political supremacy, nevertheless the second judges the link between the two elements of social hegemony to be much weaker. Given the obscurity which shrouds the origins of Rome, such an opaque and complex question cannot be resolved lightly. Nevertheless the key seems to lie in a differentiation between two successive periods, the first characterised by the overwhelming military, social and political predominance of the cavalry, the second by the introduction of hoplite armies. The aristocratic knights managed more or less to maintain their social and political superiority in the expanded civic body, but they could hardly have maintained superiority on the battlefield against a bronze wall of hoplites (except in a few peripheral regions that were late in developing or were particularly suited to cavalry tactics). The practical link between cavalry and aristocracy will then have been replaced by symbolic and honorific links in the Roman world; perhaps in most Greek cities too, where, according to Aristotle (*Politics,* IV, 1297 16–22) citizenship in the earliest republics was restricted to cavalrymen.

Be that as it may, after the development of the hoplite army, there is no doubt that the cavalry was for a long time reduced to a secondary though not negligible role in battle. In the Athenian army, in the age of Pericles, there was only one cavalryman to every thirteen infantrymen; elsewhere in Greece the ratio reached one to ten. In the following century, to be sure, more use was made of the cavalry to harass the enemy, but the effectiveness of the tactic remained a limited one. As Xenophon said to his infantry company, in order to reassure them (*Anabasis* III, 2, 18–19):

> But if any one of you is despondent because we are without horsemen while the enemy have plenty, let him reflect that ten thousand horsemen are nothing more than ten thousand men. Nobody ever lost his life in battle from the bite or kick of a horse; it is the men who do whatever is done in battles. Moreover we are on a far surer foundation than horsemen. They are hanging on their horses' backs, afraid not only of us but also of falling off while we, standing on the ground shall strike with far greater force if anyone comes upon us and shall be far more likely to hit whomever we aim at. Horsemen have only one advantage: flight is safer for them than it is for us.

Later, the number and variety of cavalrymen were increased considerably by Alexander of Macedon, who relied not only on his own compatriots, but also on Greek and barbarian allies. Two thousand Macedonian nobles were regrouped into the 'Cavalry of the Companions,' and equipped with arms which enabled them in the right circumstances to charge the enemy infantry on the flanks or in the rear. A supplementary cavalry force, carrying lighter arms than the Companions, was recruited from the rest of the Macedonian population and from the allies. But this effort of Alexander's was not repeated by the Hellenistic rulers: the ratio of the cavalry to the phalanx, often as high as one to two in his armies, fell to one to five in the Seleucid armies at the battle of Raphia (218 BC) and to one to eight in the Macedonian armies at the time of Philip V.

THE MILITARY SOCIETIES

The Romans also adopted the practice of harassment, especially from the second century BC. The burden fell largely on the allies, later on the auxiliaries, organised into independent wings, who compensated for the steady fall in the numbers of the citizen cavalry. In Polybius' time there were 200 to 300 cavalrymen in a legion, by the beginning of the Empire only 120 (serving essentially as mounted messengers). Soon, however, the pressure on the frontiers by barbarians with a long experience of their own modes of equestrian fighting, previously unknown to the Romans, compelled the latter to increase the numbers and improve the armament of their cavalry. They relied above all on federated peoples (of the same race and culture as their enemies), admitting them into the Roman army without altering their national customs.*

Similarly, from the time of the Flavians, the emperors faced with mounted bowmen from the Eurasian steppes and the Arabian and Saharan deserts, set up cavalry units, composed of Thracians, Syrians, and Numidians. The question which then arises, whether heavy cavalry developed in the west in the same way, indirectly raises the problem of the origins of the medieval knights and requires us to extend our field of enquiry somewhat. Heavy cavalry is commonly thought to have originated in Turan in central Asia. The first known appearance in action was in Assyria towards the middle of the eighth century BC, then in Chorezm (Russian Turkestan) in the sixth century. Not only were the local breeds of horses exceptional in quality (a few specimens have been preserved in the tumuli of Pazirik on the slopes of the Altai Mountains), but the nomadic societies were strongly hierarchical in structure with a privileged minority able to shoulder the costs of the equipment.

The Romans had no occasion to test this type of opponent until they came up against the Parthians, the most reputed of all the barbarian horsemen, who crushed them in 53 BC; then against the Sarmatians and the Dacians, who started to harass the Danube frontier in the second half of the first century AD. To meet these dangerous enemies on their home ground, the Romans undertook to create their own heavy cavalry gradually

* From Hadrian's time, they were organised into *cunei* with a status equivalent to that of the *numeri* of the infantry.

and cautiously, aware as they were of the disadvantages alongside the advantages. At first, probably in the reign of Vespasian, they contented themselves with increasing the striking force of some of their cavalrymen by equipping them with powerful spurs. The first cuirassiers appeared in Hadrian's time, but it seems to have been only the men who wore chain mail, not the horses, and this was often the case later among the numerous units of *cataphracti, clibanarii,* and *loricati* formed from the reign of Gallienus onwards.

On the whole, then, the Romans refused to provide their heavy cavalry with the full panoply of the barbarian cuirassiers, because their approach to cavalry was always half-hearted. Above all, the most original feature of so-called Tranian tactics —the systematic cooperation between mounted bowmen who incited the enemy to break ranks, and heavy cavalry who forced them to regroup, remained unknown to the Romans. Hence their many defeats, such as at Adrianople in 378—which did nothing to encourage them to continue experimenting. Not until the introduction and diffusion of the stirrup in the eighth century, which gave the cuirassier a firmer seat, did he acquire the striking power and autonomy of action which made it possible for the medieval knighthood to impose its military and social supremacy in the west.

This technological problem, like the one of the horse harness, brings us to one fundamental cause of the failure of the cavalry in antiquity. Another was the cost of the upkeep of horses, which only a social elite or a state devoted to war was in a position to bear. Together they explain why, despite its social prestige, the cavalry played only a secondary role in the military field, save in exceptional circumstances, and why it did not always draw the best of the fighting men.

The Primacy of the Heavy Infantry

As a general rule, then, control of territory fell to the heavy infantry, the defender *par excellence* of the agricultural plains, despite the alterations in its equipment and its tactical organisation over the centuries.

The primacy of the heavy infantry is already announced in the Homeric poems. The Achaean and Trojan champions, clad in their heavy armour, leap from their chariots, hurl cutting insults at each other, and then, before the serried ranks of the anonymous masses of infantry they launch into duels, as rhythmic and formal as sword dances, until one of the combatants (usually the Trojan) either falls or takes to his heels.

The magic of the poetry has imposed this Homeric model on our ideas of warfare among all ancient aristocratic societies preceding the invention of the hoplite phalanx, whether Mycenaean kingdoms or Italic, Thracian or Germanic tribes of the early first millennium BC. This assimilation is probably justified by and large so long as it is not forgotten that this is a poetic model aimed at emphasising the personal valour of the heroes and the omnipotence of the gods, even at the cost of certain implausibilities and contradictions. For instance it is difficult to believe in a battlefield fragmented into as many individual duelling-grounds as there were pairs of champions eager to fight it out. This tactic appears to be a confusion of two actual chronologically distinct modes of combat: an ancient Mycenaean one in which elite combatants fought in chariots, and a more recent post-Mycenaean one in which the elite, on foot, led their troops but were not isolated from them. Once the aristocrats ceased to dominate the mêlée from their chariots, it was inevitable that they would have fewer opportunities to distinguish themselves from the mass of fighting men than the poet imagined.

The hoplite, who replaced the fighters of the heroic age and dominated the battlefields for several centuries was 'defined' by his armour. He carried a round shield (*hoplon*), held by a central loop (*porpax*) which gripped the forearm near the elbow and a strap (*antilabe*) which he grasped in his hand; wore a helmet, breastplate and greaves of bronze; and was armed with a wooden lance, 2–2½ metres long, and a short sword for hand-to-hand fighting. These items of equipment appear all together for the first time on certain proto-Corinthian vases of the period 675–650 BC and some scholars concluded that the whole panoply was invented at that time in some city in the Peloponnese (Argos, Sparta, or Corinth). However the most recent archaeological discoveries suggest instead a gradual development with various tentative experiments, to which many Greek cities contributed. Thus, the earliest bronze breastplate and helmet have been found in an Argive tomb of about 725 BC, the first shields with central armhole and strap on proto-Corinthian vases and in Aegean figurines of about 700; the first greaves, on proto-Corinthian and proto-Attic vases of about 675. Their antecedents, furthermore, take us to Western Asia (Assyria and Urartu) and to central Europe and Italy, then being opened to Greek colonisation and commerce, and certain essential details such as the shieldhold as finally perfected should be credited to the Greek genius.

The introduction of the hoplite panoply is logically inseparable from the adoption of a new battle formation, the phalanx. In order to hold off the enemy at the end of their lances while protecting their right flank from enemy projectiles the hoplites had to be fighting in close formation. Moreover, to prevent an easy break in the formation, followed by a general rout, the men were drawn up several ranks deep (never less than four, normally eight). Hence, too, the necessity of engaging battle on level terrain, of bringing up troops and having them charge in waves in unison over the entire front, of keeping the rhythm of the advance steady, to overcome the tendency of each soldier to veer imperceptibly to the right, seeking the cover of his neighbour's shield. These were difficult rules to put into practice, and we find them scrupulously applied in only a few battles, such as Marathon.

The introduction of the hoplite panoply and of a battle formation founded upon a spirit of solidarity and discipline is usually associated with the birth of the city-state and the expansion of the civic body. But historians disagree over the sequence. Some believe that the technical progress in arms imposed a new battle formation and this forced the aristocracy to involve the whole citizen-body in the defence of the community, and consequently to share political power with them. Others hold, on the contrary, that a change in social relationships dispossessed the aristocracy of its political privileges and thus brought about the establishment of a battle formation which both favoured mass action and inspired the invention of appropriate armour.

When both explanations were found to be too narrow to account for all the evidence, it was suggested that the hoplite phalanx was introduced as a purely technical instrument in the service of the aristocracy, but soon became an instrument promoting advancement of new social strata; in other words, that

the aristocracy, by assuming the initiative in this military reform, was unconsciously working towards the destruction of its
own social supremacy. Although this view pays scrupulous
attention to the known facts, and especially to their chrono-
logical sequence, one cannot help wondering about the extent
to which it exploits the considerable gaps in our evidence in
order to dissolve the politico-military units of a single historical
process. The fact that the phalanx is first attested a quarter of a
century after the hoplite panoply and half a century before the
Solonic revolution does not prove that the three phenomena
were independent in aim and function. Was the link between
them in historical reality or only in the minds of modern historians? The eighth and seventh centuries were, beyond question,
periods of social tension producing a strong bias towards
tyranny. Is it credible that the hoplite phalanx, with all its
social and political implications, could have remained 'above
the battle'?

Should we not reject any suggestion that a mode of combat
is nothing but a fortuitous combination of autonomous, heterogeneous forces, technical, economic, social and political? The
hoplite phalanx should therefore be seen as both the cause and
consequence of the social changes which brought about the
progressive expansion of the civic body within the Greek city-
state, from which it diffused into a number of peripheral
regions.

From a purely technical point of view, the Macedonian
phalanx, created towards the middle of the fourth century BC
by Philip II, was one of a number of improvements in the
hoplite phalanx designed to achieve greater mobility. But it
was also an adaptation to a new source of manpower, the Macedonian peasant who could not afford the expensive arms of the
Greek hoplite and had long been used to chasing bands of lightly
armed robbers, who periodically came down to the plain from
the Balkan highlands. These peasant-soldiers were equipped
with a smaller shield than that of the hoplite, with a helmet,
metal greaves, perhaps a light breastplate, and a medium-length
sword, and they carried a lance (*sarissa*) sometimes more than
six metres long. They were grouped in battalions (*taxeis*) of
about 1,500 men, usually drawn up in ranks sixteen deep, of
which only the first five were directly engaged in battle. In the

course of the Hellenistic period their arms tended to become heavier with a consequent loss of manoeuvrability; by the time the Macedonian phalanx came up against the Roman legion, it was as cumbersome as the old Greek hoplite phalanx.

The Roman legion was also a descendant of the Greek phalanx, but so deeply marked by local tradition from its very beginning, so receptive to the lessons of experience during its long years of development, so powerfully endowed with such an impulse to perfection that it must count as an original Roman creation.

In the beginning, the way the men were positioned on the battlefield, probably in ranks six deep, took into account the quality of their arms, itself determined by their property assessment (*census*). The front line was filled by men of the first class, whose arms were of the hoplite type as far back as the sixth century. In the fourth century fundamental changes were introduced in response to the tactics of the Samnite highlanders. The census continued as the basis for recruitment but was abandoned as a factor of organisation in the field. Henceforth soldiers were assigned to their posts according to age rather than social status; the younger men formed the front line of *hastati*, the mature men the second line of *principes*, and the older men a third line of *triarii* or *pilani*. Even the terminology was dissociated from differences in arms, which were now more or less the same for all—an articulated and relatively light breastplate, greaves, metal helmet, an oval shield (*scutum*) of leather, reinforced with bronze on a wooden frame, and a sword of one type or another. The two front lines also carried one or two heavy javelins (*pilum*), the *triarii* or *pilani* a lance (*hasta*) similar to that of the hoplites. This type of legion consisted of sixty centuries, regrouped into thirty maniples on the battlefield.

Although the maniple formation proved successful in dislocating the rigid front of the Macedonian phalanx, it later found itself threatened in the west by the striking force of the barbarian hordes, especially Iberian, Numidian and Germanic, who fought in small units. This was no doubt the principle reason why the Romans progressively adopted a closer formation during the course of the second century BC. From this time, each legion comprised ten cohorts, each usually subdivided into three maniples, the *hastati*, the *principes* and the *triarii*. Although there were further alterations in equipment and tactics, the basic principles of the legion, then remained fundamentally the same until the second century AD, when this traditional instrument of Roman might began to deteriorate.

By the Late Empire the legions had lost their characteristic organisation, arms and tactics. They came to resemble the auxiliary units and to return from the maniple formation to the old phalanx. Negatively, this change can be explained in part by the disorganisation of the traditional army cadres. More significantly however, it was a response to new tactical and strategic conditions, to the need to stand up to barbarians who attacked without manoeuvring, relying upon their shock tactics or their ability to infiltrate the ranks; and to the need to adapt their fighting formations to the demands of self-defence.

Nevertheless the heavy infantry remained the core of the armed forces. Thus, to the end of the classical period the Greeks were loath to concentrate in the fortified town in their engagements, and they failed to develop siege techniques more effective than investment. Control of territory remained their essential objective and military potential was organised accordingly. The situation changed in the fourth century BC when such empire builders as Dionysius the Elder of Syracuse and the kings of Macedon felt it necessary to guarantee possession of the urban centres and equipped themselves with the men and material required. Siegecraft then reached its peak rapidly under Demetrius Poliorcetes of Macedon; conversely, so did the art of fortification, culminating, towards the end of the third century BC in the time of Philo of Byzantium. In this domain the Romans were mere imitators, although, it is true, capable of acting with quite exceptional energy.

The Light-Armed Troops

Throughout antiquity the heavy infantry, whatever its battle formation, was always flanked by a variable number of light-armed troops relying principally on missiles: bows, slings, javelins and even ordinary stones thrown by hand (the use of which should not be underestimated). However, despite their skill and their ability to adapt to the terrain, the light infantry was discredited by the tradition of being reserved for those second class fighters who were unable to pay for, or deemed unworthy of

127

bearing, a full panoply, and they had difficulty in imposing themselves on the battlefield, except when the heavy infantry was inadequate or in decline.

In Greece bowmen, slingers, and throwers of stones or javelins appear to have become increasingly important from early times into the Mycenaean period, and to have remained important until the eighth century BC. Then the hoplites appeared on the scene and reduced the light troops to the secondary functions of opening a battle with a few preliminary skirmishes and of acting as scouts. The use of the bow now came to be regarded as incompatible with the values and practices of a hoplite. For example, it was forbidden in the Lelantine War (usually dated at the end of the eighth or the beginning of the seventh century), condemned by the poet Archilochus in the middle of the seventh century, and considered a barbarian weapon in the Persian wars. In Euripides' *Heracles* (II, 162–4), it was the theme of a debate the outcome of which was not in its favour:

> The bow is no proof of manly courage;
> no, your real man stands firm in the ranks
> and dares to face the gash the spear may make.

But the very fact of disagreement shows that this condemnation was no longer absolute. And from the fourth century light-armed soldiers of various kinds proliferated. Their equipment became widely varied for, in place of the poorer citizens, it was now possible to call upon barbarian and semi-barbarian peoples of the Balkans and Asia, and there was every reason to preserve their traditional modes of combat.

The Romans also started by recruiting their light troops (*velites*) among the lower social strata. After the 'Servian reform' they were organised in twenty-five centuries from the fourth and fifth classes. By the time of Polybius, however, the majority were drawn from the Italian allies (*socii*), organised into 'wings' (*alae*) independent of the legions, and posted at the extremities in the battle formation. Still later, when the theatre of operations moved out of Italy and when, after the Social War, Italians were admitted into the legions, Rome acquired an inexhaustible source of native auxiliaries serving as allies or mercenaries and retaining their own national arms.

From the time of Augustus the auxiliaries, as numerous as

the legionary soldiers, made up permanent units with increasingly complex composition, functions and equipment. In the
following century Hadrian joined to the auxiliary infantry
cohorts other formations (*numeri*) who retained more of their
national characteristics, and were thus in a better position to
meet the barbarians on their own terms. In the Late Empire the
majority of the infantry units were more or less amalgamated
with the *numeri*, leading to an extremely confused situation in
which the ancient legions, now technically retrograde, were indistinguishable from those barbarian units which had adopted
their armament, and found themselves swamped by alien
national contingents faithful to their own traditional modes of
combat.

In sum, when confronted with barbarian hordes, the ancient
infantry ended by a kind of local mimicry. Such a tendency, it
should be noted, had always been felt on the margins of the
Greco-Roman world—in the Greek colonies on the Black Sea,
and in the western Mediterranean, for example, or along the
Asiatic and African frontiers of the Roman Empire, where
relatively strong bodies of bowmen had been maintained all
along.

Seamen

In many respects the status of sailors was similar to that of
the light-armed infantrymen. To be sure, a few ancient states
were able to maintain a strong navy, more or less temporarily:
classical Athens, Hellenistic Egypt and Rhodes, Rome during
the Punic Wars and again at the end of the Republic. It is also
true that certain naval battles, Salamis in the second Persian
War, Aegospotami at the end of the Peloponnesian War, the
Egadi Islands in the first Punic War, or Actium in the struggle
between Augustus and Antony, had a determining influence on
the course of events. And, given the level of technology in antiquity, one must acknowledge the exceptional quality of their
warships.

However, to assess the historical significance of these facts
one must set them within the general context of military affairs.
In particular, one must try to assess the relative importance of
organisation and improvisation, of deliberate choice and mere
chance. The Romans, it has been remarked, 'sought to conquer

the sea from the land'; and 'the naval policy of Rome was to avoid the need of having one'; the consummation of Roman naval policy was reached when the Mediterranean could at last be made not so much a sea as a Roman lake.'*

Although it would be paradoxical to say the same of the Greeks for whom geography made it essential to come to terms with the sea, one should avoid hasty generalisations and anachronisms. In the first place, it is not a question of the 'Greeks' but of certain Greek states who, at particular moments in their history, used the navy as the essential instrument of military power. The majority, like the Romans, always treated the navy as subordinate. Second, supremacy at sea was never enough in itself in antiquity as it has been in modern times, when a blockade of the coast and the interruption of commercial relations have played a determining role in our conflicts. Ancient navies were employed basically for territorial expansion, their ultimate aim and the necessary condition for their existence.

Technically, war at sea had its own specific conditions. For example, before modern artillery made long-range combat possible, warships had to be 'long' ships propelled by oars, and thus radically different from 'round' merchant vessels relying on sails. Furthermore, from the seventh century BC until the third century AD, the oarsmen were normally stationed on two or three levels, one above the other (biremes and triremes) and in such conditions the ability to manoeuvre the ships required a long training. Certain contradictions followed between the technological originality of maritime activity and its inferiority, in principle, to activity on land; between the high qualifications of sailors and their low military status (with the exception of the marines, always equal in rank to the elite of the land forces.)

In the classical period the Athenians manned their ships by choice with citizens of the lowest census class, the *thetes*. Only in moments of danger, as on the eve of the battle of Salamis, did they call upon the *zeugites* and the knights as well, just as they often turned to their allies, especially during the Empire and sometimes even to mercenaries. The Hellenistic sovereigns recruited men for pay from among their subjects or among the

---

* F. E. Adcock, *The Roman Art of War Under the Republic* (Cambridge 1960), 31, 37 and 47 respectively.

experienced seamen of the Aegean, in Asia Minor, Cyprus and Phoenicia. By then there were few Greek cities, such as Rhodes, which still clung to the principle of using their own citizens.

Unlike the Greeks, who had accepted the need to take an oar in defence of their country and had at times even been proud to do so, Roman citizens always felt naval service to be beneath their dignity, except in the ranks of the marines. Their rightful place was in the legions, not as galley fodder. During the Republic sailors and rowers therefore had to be recruited among the marginal elements, at a pinch citizens from the maritime colonies, but usually from freedmen and above all, in increasing proportions, from the allies. The latter either entered directly into service in the Roman fleet or had to supply auxiliary squadrons. It is significant that the term *socii navales* (naval allies) soon came to designate all Roman crews whatever their origin. The incompatibility in principle between citizenship and service in the navy was felt so strongly that as soon as the Italians acquired Roman citizenship in 90–89, they ceased to belong to the *socii navales*. Pompey, Brutus, Cassius and Antony were therefore obliged to recruit their crews in the civil wars outside Italy, while Sextus Pompey and even Octavius were reduced to calling upon slaves.

The situation remained unchanged during the Empire, at least until the edict of Caracalla of 212 AD which extended citizenship generally and stripped it of most of its significance. Although one should not exaggerate the number of freedmen who entered the Roman navy in the early Principate, let alone that of slaves, and although sailors often adopted Latin names from the time of Vespasian, they retained their status of aliens (*peregrini*) until the end of the second century AD. Many, of Egyptian origin, were in an even more inferior position and hardly a single Roman or Italian is to be found amongst them (unless for disciplinary reasons). In the hierarchy of military and civic values the difference between the sailor and the legionary was a difference in kind, not only in degree: the sailor was only a marginal member of the community of arms.

Similarly, the ancients rarely developed and elaborated their naval tactics to the same level as their land tactics; nor did their tactics attain as high a degree of professionalism as their naval construction. Here, too, the chief reason presumably lies in the prestige of land warfare, in contrast to the suspicion, even the discredit, more or less marked in different periods, attached to maritime operations, whatever their actual contribution to the outcome of war.

Obviously no-one, in the age of Pericles, would have dreamed of denying that control of the sea was the basis of Athenian imperialism. By projecting that situation into the past, some writers interpreted older Greek history as a succession of thalassocracies. But, to contemporary oligarchs at least, the maritime base of Athens' strength appeared as the main cause of the moral and political disintegration which would bring about the city's downfall. Such a city, they argued, was at the mercy of the naval plebs who would inevitably force it towards the most extreme forms of democracy. The 'excesses' of the demagogues who succeeded Pericles and then the defeat by Sparta in 404 encouraged the diffusion of such oligarchical views in the conservative thought of the fourth century. Both Isocrates and Xenophon saw maritime supremacy as a source of injustice, idleness, avarice, envy and eventually tyranny. Plato was careful to locate his ideal city away from the sea lest it should succumb to the temptation. Appeals to the glorious military past tended to emphasise the victory at Marathon at the expense of Salamis.

When the heat of this debate was tempered by the decline of Athens' naval ambitions, the criticisms became less severe and more marked. Aristotle and later Cicero were equally sensitive to the poisonous influences emanating from harbours but they were prepared to accept a compromise for reasons of military and economic efficiency. The new genre of literary 'eulogies' even took account of the advantages of the sea. However, the rehabilitation was limited and insecure. The moment national animosity came into the picture, like that of the Romans for the Carthaginians, the traditional insults were trotted out again without scruple.

The subordination of sea warfare was thus a matter of political values. The alternative not only created the risk of ruining the traditional landed base of the economy more or less rapidly, but also forced an increase in the political rights of the lower classes who provided the naval manpower. Hypothetically one might argue that the social elite could have taken its place in the navy. However, that would disregard both the extent to which their economic status rested on exploitation of the land and the weight of ideological prejudice.

In a sense, a fundamental incompatibility emerged between the traditional political structures of the city and the growth of naval warfare. The latter depended so heavily on the quality of the equipment and the professional skill of the men that it threatened to turn military activity into a technical or occupational one (at a time when the profession of arms was still fairly unsophisticated in land warfare). It therefore seemed preferable to leave such military activity to the marginal people in the political life of the community; otherwise, since naval service was not consistent with the traditional identification of the soldier with the citizen, the navy might well have had an undermining effect on the social hierarchy and have challenged some of the fundamental principles of the city.

The relationships between the socio-political status of the fighting men and their military status were extremely complex in the course of ancient history. The rise of different modes of combat obviously depended on the material basis, itself determined by the state of the productive sources, but that merely defines the limits of possibility in the abstract. In their concrete historical manifestations the military societies bore the imprint of their social structures, both real and ideal, of the political circumstances which conditioned their formation, and of the inner logic of the modes of combat they created.

Army Organisation

The increasingly technical nature of warfare, combined with the extension of the fields of operation and the growth of professionalism, provoked so spectacular a development in army organisation that the military institutions of the Roman Empire remained a model into the modern age.

THE MATERIAL CONDITIONS

The rigid framework of the ancient economy created difficult, precarious and often artificial conditions for larger, genuinely urban committees. Once their needs outgrew the resources of their own territory, the surplus agricultural produce they required to feed themselves could be obtained only by imposing a vast system of compulsory contributions or by establishing an extended network of commercial relations served by adequate means of transport. Ancient armies, being non-productive by definition, faced analogous problems, although formulated somewhat differently because their objectives and their methods were determined by strictly military imperatives.

Supply Corps and Camp Followers

The administrative structures of ancient states were usually inadequate to ensure army supply. Therefore the armies were forced to develop on their own all the services necessary for their survival, and this they accomplished by employing a considerable number of non-combatants. Even before the increase in military mechanisation brought about a corresponding growth in equipment and the creation of a specialised corps of engineers, it was necessary in the interest of efficiency that each Greek hoplite and cavalryman be accompanied on campaign by one or more personal attendants. The evidence goes back to the Persian wars (not to mention the Homeric period), but the practice presumably increased in the fourth century, when bands of mercenaries, veritable cities on the move, tended to surround themselves with all the conveniences of civil life.

As campaigns began to last longer and armies became professionalised, the need was felt to allow soldiers to have their families accompany them. The state itself rarely undertook to provide women, as Pericles is said to have done in 440–439 BC: 'The Samian cult of Aphrodite, known by some as the cult of the reeds and by others as cult of the marshes, was introduced by the Athenian prostitutes who accompanied Pericles at the siege of Samos; as it turned out, they did good business.'* Normally, the soldiers themselves took the initiative: in the baggage trains, alongside the booty, were to be found their women and children, sometimes attended by personal slaves. Together with scavengers, hangers-on and entertainers of every kind, they formed huge convoys which considerably hampered army movements and made the manoeuvres seem more like migrations than military expeditions. But this love of family and attachment to the pleasures of life were at the same time the best guarantees of the troops' loyalty and fighting spirit; among the mercenary troops a way of compensating for the absence of patriotism.

The Romans were more effective than the Greeks, with armies on the move, in checking the proliferation of campfollowers whose only function was to contribute, directly or indirectly, to the well-being of the fighting men. However, they too never seriously considered putting a stop to it in garrisons. Although the early emperors forbade soldiers in service from marrying, they tolerated 'illegal' unions and granted a privileged status even to the concubines and illegitimate children of soldiers, including, above all, the right to legal recognition and, if the head of the family was a legionary, citizenship, when the term of military service was completed. From the time of Septimius Severus, a soldier's family life was officially recognised, an innovation followed by a steady increase in both private housing (*canabae*) and places of public recreation on the periphery of the camps.

* Alexis of Samos.

Health Services

Very often the creature comforts of the soldiers in the ancient armies were better taken care of than their health. Military medical services were late to develop; at least, it was a long time before they formed a proper service as distinct from private initiative. Until the end of the classical period in Greece, and equally in the Roman Republic, the state, while extending its protection to war victims (orphans and cripples), showed little concern for the sick and wounded during campaigns. The responsibility fell to the soldiers themselves, to friendly cities in the neighbourhood, to the personal doctors of the generals or the ambulant doctors (often of doubtful reputation) who followed armies on the move. Hellenistic mercenaries, however, less prepared than citizens to pay with their life-blood, began to insist upon attention and guarantees from their employers. Philo of Byzantium recommends (V, 3, 45–48; 72–73):

> If there are any wounded among the foreigners, they must be looked after with care and provided with all they need. Those among them who have nobody to care for them must be placed in the houses of citizens . . . If any of them die they must be buried with as much ceremony as possible at the expense of the community, and if they leave children or wives behind, these must be looked after scrupulously. This is the best way to instil in them loyalty to the generals and citizens, so that they confront danger bravely . . . There must also be on the spot excellent doctors, skilled in healing wounds and extracting missiles, equipped with the appropriate medicines and instruments, and provided by the city with ointments, honey, bandages and lint, not only to prevent the wounded from dying but also to render them, having rapidly recovered their health, useful in subsequent encounters, being ready to court danger in the knowledge that they had been healed and well looked after. This often ensures the salvation of a city.

Medical services progressively improved in Rome during the first century BC, but it was only under the Empire that doctors were officially attached to the armed forces. They ranked as *immunes* or *principales* and were placed, together with their male nurses, under the direct command of the camp prefect responsible for servicing the garrison. There was a hospital (*valetudinarium*) in each camp, a large building with an inner court surrounded by corridors with sometimes as many as sixty rooms. The numerous surgical instruments discovered by archaeologists in military establishments and the scope of their sanitary installations (taps for drinking water, baths, latrines) all testify to the attention given to physical condition in the imperial armies. In the end, then, the state assumed what had long been the responsibility of individual initiative and private charity.

Food Supply

'An army marches on its stomach', Napoleon is supposed to have said, and it is quite true that the quality of the catering has always been an essential condition for the morale and efficiency of armed forces. This condition was more difficult to fulfil in ancient societies than in modern Europe, for techniques of production, distribution and storage were inferior, the administrative apparatus less developed and usually incompetent in economic matters, while, conversely, the numbers of soldiers and troop concentrations, which could reach fifty thousand, were often as great as in modern times.

The basic ration was grain: about a litre and a quarter of wheat a day (which gave just under a kilogram and a half of bread, biscuit or porridge), some of which might be replaced by barley in times of shortage or as a punishment. This *sitos* (Greek) or *frumentum* (Latin) was complemented by *opsonion* or *commeatus*: meat, which varied according to circumstances in quantity and form (fresh, salted or smoked); cheese; vegetables (mostly onions in Greece), and salt. As for beverage, the Greek preference was wine, replaced among the Romans, at least while engaged in operations, by *posca*, a mixture of water and vinegar.

Short expeditions into neighbouring territories could, of course, be managed on the provisions with which each soldier equipped himself before leaving home. Foraging then helped them to improve on their basic rations, and, when necessary, to prolong the campaign. According to Homer, the Achaeans were able to subsist beneath the walls of Troy by raiding the northern coasts of the Aegean Sea, without being compelled, contrary to what Thucydides supposed (I, 11, 1) to cultivate the Chersonese.

To the end of antiquity, armies always tried to live off the land, as far as possible. But this procedure was both delicate and risky. Politically, it was not to be recommended if there were any reason for keeping on the right side of the local population. From the military point of view it was dangerous because it temporarily reduced the number of fighting men available, and in the long run led to anarchy and lack of discipline. Finally, from the economic point of view, its efficiency could only be short-lived even if the enemy refrained from adopting a scorched earth policy. Both Greeks and Romans were consequently obliged to control the application of such a policy, just as they had to regulate the collection of booty. According to Polyaenus (III, 10, 5), Timotheus, the Greek general of the first half of the fourth century BC, proceeded in the following manner:

> Having set up his camp around a city, he indicated the limits of the area which his troops could pillage; the rest of the territory and everything of use in it was sold. He did not allow harvests or farms to be destroyed nor fruit trees to be felled, though the fruit could be gathered. The advantages he derived were as follows: if he was victorious his gains were increased, and if the war dragged on food and lodging were available in abundance. Even more important, he thus won considerable support from the enemy population.

If one was unable or unwilling to depend upon pillaging, an alternative system of supply was necessary. The most obvious and most effective was to make the state responsible, but in the Greece of the city-states the state was particularly ill-equipped to do so in any continuous fashion. Besides, unless there happened to be allied peoples near by who were willing to take responsibility, food shipments were, for technological reasons, difficult to organise on land, or even by sea in the stormy season.

Nevertheless there are a few examples from the fifth century BC. In 479, on the eve of the battle of Plataea, a train of five hundred mules bringing food from the Peloponnese for the army was caught by the Persian cavalry lying in ambush in the passes of Mt. Cithaeron (Herodotus, IX, 39). At the end of the summer of 425, the Athenians became concerned for their garrison of Pylos on the west coast of the Peloponnese, which was blockading Sphacteria. They 'began to fear', according to Thucydides (IV, 27, 1) 'that winter might come on and find them still engaged in the blockade. They saw that the convoying of provisions round the Peloponnese would be then impossible. The country offered no real resources in itself and even in summer they could not send round enough.' In 415, the Athenians made provision from the start for their expeditionary force to Sicily. 'The supplies for this force were carried by thirty ships of burden laden with corn, which conveyed the bakers, stone masons and carpenters, and the tools for raising fortifications, accompanied by one hundred boats, like the former pressed into service, besides many other boats and ships of burden which followed the armament voluntarily for purposes of trade' (Thucydides VI, 44, 1).

But this was not yet a genuine, permanent commissary service under the sole control of the military authorities. Such a degree of organisation was reached, to some extent, only much later, if not in the armies of Philip and Alexander, at least during the Hellenistic period. For instance, a remark made by Strabo (XVI, 2, 10) suggests that at one time there existed in the Seleucid kingdom a catering corps of paid employees under a secretary-general.

The clearest evidence comes from garrison towns. There the responsibility for amassing reserves of food (especially grain) fell either to the regular civic officials or to the leaders of the occupying troops. The latter were bound by certain rules, an example of which, dating from the end of the third century BC, has been discovered in an underground chamber in the fortress of Chalcis in Euboea:

> The *oeconomi* shall see to it that the king's orders concerning the stores are exactly kept. Existing stores which have been measured shall be measured again in the presence of the garrison commanders, and all those whose weight has been taken shall be weighed again so that the garrison commanders should also know what there is there. The keys of the storehouses shall be held by the agents of the *oeconomi*. The garrison commanders shall seal the chambers and shall take care that nothing be removed from the

stocks except whatever appears to be rotten on account of its age, and this they shall remove only after having admitted the equivalent quantity. They shall take in wheat, dried, from the last harvest and immediately order that it be sprinkled with Chalcidian earth, and they shall make sure of the quality of the wine and of the wood every four years, and take care to take in wine of the year, sweet and tasted. They shall also inspect the wheat granaries: during the six months of summer each time it has rained, and every ten days during the winter. And if there has been a leak of water into the wheat repairs shall be made forthwith.

If any *oeconomi* or employers of the *oeconomi* remove the seals without the permission of the garrison commander or withdraw something without having taken in the equivalent, or, through not having made inspections at the appointed time, allow certain products to deteriorate they shall, after an enquiry, suffer the punishment prescribed by the king. If the garrison commanders neglect the supervision of the stocks—whether they have voluntarily delegated to someone else or whether they are personally responsible—they shall be liable to the punishment prescribed by the king. If the *oeconomi* fail to execute any of the prescriptions contained in this order the garrison commander in charge of the place where the negligence has occurred shall write immediately to the king so that the king shall decide what punishment the author of this negligence merits. If he does not send a letter before the king is informed about it by someone else, he shall pay a fine of six thousand drachmas.

Each of the *oeconomi* shall have this order transcribed on to a stele and erected in the spot most visible from the garrison, and he shall undertake personally when he is transferred to another post or discharged from the service, to entrust it to his successor at the same time as everything else which is connected with his function as *oeconomus*, in accordance with this order.*

* C. B. Welles, 'New texts from the chancery of Philip V of Macedonia and the problem of the *diagramma*', *American Journal of Archaeology*, 42 (1938) pp. 251–254.

However, such a text should not persuade us that there was complete state control over military provisioning even in the garrison towns. For one thing, the economic role played by the city or by the general did not free the individual soldier from having to buy his own rations with money, and he could thus fall victim to speculations engaged in by his own employer. Nor was private enterprise completely eliminated. It is significant, in particular, that Philo of Byzantium, also writing at the end of the third century BC, tells us that, apart from the grain which had to be 'set aside in storage at least once a year' by the city, most of the provisioning remained in the hands of private individuals. These were, in the main, rich citizens, in whose houses 'shall be stored dried meats and meats preserved in the dregs of the wine, and also salt meats', or sometimes the specialised professional groups, the cooks, for example, when it was a matter of laying in pork livers 'salted and dried in the shade' in accordance with a decree (V, 2, 1–5).

Even during the Hellenistic period, furthermore, armies campaigning far afield continued as before to depend essentially upon the services of local merchants who, either of their own free will or under compulsion, were resigned to doing business with the visitors; or else upon merchants who, having sometimes travelled long distances for the purpose, gravitated round the campaigning armies either on their own initiative or at the behest of the generals. However, the armies were not wholly at the mercy of the merchants, wholesale or retail, who were always inclined to take advantage of circumstances. These special markets were strictly supervised by the military authorities who would subsequently be responsible for apportioning the booty. Sometimes they appointed market overseers, or intervened, for instance, to increase the supply of ready cash by artificial means, most often to impose price controls in order to protect the soldiers' purse and prevent discontent.

Roman armies in the late Republic adopted similar solutions, although there was a more closely linked network of provisioning bases. The baggage train and commissariat were also better organised, the responsibility of a quaestor in each legion, with a greater autonomy of action when necessary. But on the whole there was little differentiation among the various technical services in the army until Augustus placed military provisioning, the military *annona,* under the control of the central financial bureau and developed a proper catering corps. In each province the responsibility rested with the governor and the financial procurator who had available bureaux staffed by imperial slaves or freedmen and by superior officers detailed to special convoys. Catering services were set up in each army corps, composed of *actuarii, curatores* and *optiones* who were in charge of the receipt and distribution of provisions. However, the public granaries, stocked by ordinary taxes, sometimes paid in kind, could supply only a portion of the necessary provisions; for the rest, traditional methods were resorted to: requisitioning in time of war, more generally, compelling cities to feed and billet troops on the march; the purchases of grain at prices fixed by the state; the cultivation by native farmers or even by the soldiers themselves, of land reserved for the upkeep of each unit.

The problems loomed even larger from the third century AD, when the practice of giving in kind became general. The *annona* was then progressively transformed into a special tax, paid in kind. At first localised and exceptional, it became increasingly common, until it was fully institutionalised by Diocletian. Under Constantine, finally, it was stripped of its military association and became the chief fiscal device, rudimentary but convenient, available to the later emperors for the running of the vast state machine.

Each army corps, then, either received the *annona* contributed by the region in which it was stationed or collected supplies from granaries (*mansiones*) strung out along the principal routes of communication. Their autonomy with respect to provisions was thus greatly increased and their political independence from the central power, too, all the more since those defending the frontiers (and likewise the barbarian contingents installed in the provinces) were being transformed into peasant-soldiers, more or less able to provide for their own needs.

The Supply of Arms

Throughout antiquity the problem of supplying arms was posed in the same terms. For a long time the responsibility lay with the individuals themselves, as is apparent from a passage in the *Hellenica* (III, 4, 17) in which Xenophon describes the pre-

parations, at Ephesus, of the troops under King Agesilaus of
Sparta, in 395 BC:

> The market was full of all sorts of horses and weapons,
> offered for sale, and the copper-workers, carpenters, smiths,
> leather-cutters and painters were all engaged in making
> martial weapons, so that one might have thought that the
> city was really a workshop of war.

When the responsibility eventually fell to the state it did so by
deducting the cost from the soldiers' pay, for ideological as well
as economic reasons. Dionysius the Elder, tyrant of Syracuse,
was apparently one of the first to take the arms 'industry' directly in hand. At a critical moment in his struggle against the Carthaginians (at the beginning of the fourth century BC) Diodorus
reports (XIV, 41, 3–42, 2):

> He gathered skilled workmen, commandeering them from
> the cities under his control and attracted them by high
> wages from Italy and Greece as well as Carthaginian terri-
> tory. For his purpose was to make weapons in great num-
> bers, and every kind of missile, and also quadriremes and
> quinquiremes, no ship of the latter size having yet been
> built at that time. After collecting many skilled workmen
> he divided them into groups in accordance with their skills,
> and appointed over them the most conspicuous citizens,
> offering great bounties to any one who created a supply of
> arms. As for the armour, he distributed among them models
> of each kind, because he had gathered his mercenaries from
> many nations; for he was eager to have every one of his
> soldiers armed with the weapons of his people, conceiving
> that by such armour his army would, for this very reason,
> cause great consternation, and that in battle all of his
> soldiers would fight to best effect in armour to which they
> were accustomed.
>
> And since the Syracusans enthusiastically supported the
> policies of Dionysius it came to pass that rivalry rose high
> to manufacture the arms. For not only was every space,
> such as the porticoes and backrooms of the temples as well
> as the gymnasia and colonnades of the market place
> crowded with workers, but the making of arms went on

143

apart from such public places in the most distinguished homes. In fact, the catapult was invented at this time in Syracuse, since the ablest skilled workers had been gathered from everywhere into one place. The high wages as well as the numerous prizes offered to the workmen who were judged to be the best stimulated their zeal. And over and above these factors, Dionysius circulated daily among the workers, conversed with them in kindly fashion and rewarded the most zealous among them with gifts and invited them to his table. Consequently the workmen brought unsurpassable devotion to the devising of many missiles and engines of war that were strange and capable of rendering great service.

Most Greek cities, not being in a position to undertake a war effort of this magnitude, had to call on private enterprise in times of need, although they were quite prepared to stimulate production temporarily by authoritarian means. Only the most powerful and best organised of the Hellenistic kingdoms were able to establish more or less permanent state arsenals capable of supplying all the arms necessary for large-scale expeditions.

In the Roman Empire, the petty craftsmen began, at a relatively early date to feel the competition from the legionary workshops run by the camp prefects, but it was only under Diocletian that genuine imperial workshops were set up, under the direct control of the central administration. Some forty are known at the beginning of the fifth century. In some respects they actually foreshadow the modern factory: production was more or less specialised and there was a high concentration of labour; there were several hundred workers in the factories of Corstopitum (Corbridge) in Britain, for example. Imperial stud farms were developed at the same time.

On the whole, the imperial armies tended not only to manufacture their own tools and utensils, but also to prepare the materials which went into them. They were thus aiming at the economic self-sufficiency which the late military writer, Vegetius (II, 11), judged to be indispensable for efficient functioning:

The legion had in its train joiners, masons, carpenters, smiths, painters, and many workers of this kind; their function was to construct lodgings and barracks for the soldiers in the winter quarters, to build mobile towers, repair chariots and war machines, and construct new ones. Various workshops responsible for making the shields, javelins, helmets, breastplates, arrows and all kinds of offensive and defensive weapons also followed the legions; for the ancients took particular care that in the camps there should never be anything lacking which might be necessary to an army.

THE EXERCISE OF COMMAND

As we saw earlier, the close tie between political standing and military rank was maintained in one form or another throughout antiquity. But warfare became more and more technical. How far was it then possible to satisfy the technical requirements without abandoning the conception of the practice of arms as a social function, without 'depoliticising' the military, by reducing it to just another service? This is the fundamental question posed by the exercise of command at the upper level of the military hierarchy.

In Homeric times the art of command had a beautiful simplicity (as no doubt in early Rome, too) which is not to denigrate it. A chieftain was expected, above all, to march at the head of his men, seeking the opportunity for a model and decisive duel in full view of his troops. He was the protagonist, the spearhead of his army. His position required that he prove the might of his arm and pay with his life, if necessary. That was how he demonstrated to both gods and men his aptitude for command. If he enjoyed a reputation for wisdom, he would also have taken care, beforehand, to draw up his troops skilfully as did wise old Nestor:

> First he arrayed the horsemen with their horses and chariots, and behind them the infantry, many and brave, to be a bulwark of battle; but the cowards he drove into the centre, that every man, however unwilling, must of necessity fight. (*Iliad*, IV 297–300).

However, it was only with the appearance of the phalanx that this task of organisation, of conditioning the ranks physically and mentally, became the prime preoccupation of the commander. It was his duty to bring his men to the battlefield in favourable conditions, to draw them up in an effective formation and to urge them on, at the last moment, by an appropriate speech delivered with all the power at his disposal, giving free rein to the ardour of his civic sentiments. There his role as general and tactician came to an end, for as soon as hostilities were opened he invariably lost control of the situation. The one way he could himself take an active part in the battle was to join the front line (usually on the right wing, where the battle was decided), and perform notable exploits and even seek a glorious death. Such conduct seemed all the more natural because it followed the old aristocratic traditions which long remained alive among the social elite.

For reasons connected with the development of military techniques (the development of the phalanx, the use of cavalry and light armed troops, the establishment of reserve corps) and with the decline of the 'agonistic' spirit in favour of cunning, surprise and treachery, it eventually became preferable for the commander to delay the moment of his own personal commitment in the battle. Xenophon appears to have been the first Greek to formulate, in consequence, a more complex, and in some respects more demanding, theory of command. He drew upon his own experience as a mercenary, upon the liberal education of the Sophists and upon the moral precepts of Socrates. Torn as he was between his attachment to tradition and his feeling for new developments, he inevitably arrived at a compromise. He asked himself whether the foremost quality of a general is bravery, as was thought in ancient times, or reflection which may enable the weaker to triumph over the stronger. His answer is that it is best to be brave, for the example it gives, but not rash, so as not to endanger the general safety for reasons of personal glory. In this way the commander would be able to win the day by making the most of circumstances.*

Later theorists lay even more emphasis upon the general's duty to ensure his own safety. This, for instance, is the advice given by Philo of Byzantium to the leader of a besieging army (V, 4, 28 and 68–69):

* C. J. N. Wood, 'Xenophon's theory of leadership', *C & M* (1964), pp. 33–66.

It is your duty not to take part in the battle, for whatever you may accomplish by spilling your own blood could not compare with the harm you would do to your interests as a whole if anything happened to you . . . Keeping yourself out of range of missiles, or moving along the lines without exposing yourself, exhort the soldiers, distribute praise and honours to those who prove their courage and berate and punish the cowards: in this way all your soldiers will confront danger as well as possible.

Compare Polybius' opinion (X, 13, 1–5) of the talent of Scipio Africanus at the siege of Carthage:

Though throwing himself heartily into the struggle, he took all possible precautions to protect his life. He had three men with him, carrying large shields which they held in such a position as to protect him completely from the side of the wall; and accordingly he went along the lines, or mounted on elevated ground and contributed greatly to the success of the day. For he was enabled to see all that was going on, and at the same time, by being himself in the view of all, inspired great zeal in the hearts of the combatants. The result was that nothing was omitted which could contribute to the success of the battle; but any help he saw to be at any moment required was rapidly and thoroughly supplied.

The same advice, finally, is found in the treatise of Onasander in the first century (XXXIII, 1–3):

The general should fight cautiously rather than boldly, or should keep away altogether from a hand-to-hand fight with the enemy. For even if in battle he shows that he is not to be outdone in valour, he can aid his army far less by fighting than he can harm it if he should be killed, since the knowledge of a general is far more important than his physical strength. Even a soldier can perform a great deed of bravery, but no one except the general can by his wisdom plan a greater one. If a ship's captain, leaving the helm, should himself do what the sailors ought to do, he would endanger his ship; in the same way, if a general, leaving his function of wise direction, should descend to the duties of a simple soldier, his neglect of the whole situation due to his lack of governing, will render useless the common soldier's mere routine service. Similar, I think, is the notion which the general gets into his heart when he thus disregards the welfare of his whole force in the event of accident to himself; for if he, with whom the safety of the whole army lies, has no care lest he himself should die, he prefers that everyone else should die with him, and rightly he would be censured as an unsuccessful rather than a courageous general.

On the other hand, this persistent stress on the prudence of the commander on the battlefield, implies that such an attitude did not seem natural. His authority continued, as in the past, to rest largely on the glory conferred by his individual exploits, physical courage and direct confrontation with the enemy. Hence, in the whole of antiquity there is not a single general who systematically abstained, who did not feel it necessary, at least on occasion, to demonstrate his personal qualities by some prestigious action, whether, like Alexander the Great, he insisted upon doing so in every decisive battle, or whether, like Scipio Africanus, he judged it sufficient to remind his soldiers of some exploit of his youth.

The qualities required of a good general changed with his role on the battlefield. So long as he remained essentially a leader of men, more stress was laid on his social standing, which guaranteed his loyalty and courage, than on his technical skills. In the last analysis, the choice of commander depended upon civic criteria identical to those which, on a more general level, determined the standing of the combatants.

The commander's intellectual qualities began to be a serious consideration only when prudence became his cardinal virtue, in Greece about the middle of the classical period. Xenophon tried to define them, but as a good Socratic, he failed to distinguish them clearly from moral qualities, which were themselves more or less a function of social status. Plato then succeeded in defining leadership more precisely, in technical terms. He saw the military art merely as an instrument in the service of politics, as an empirical art; it required courage, of course, but also long experience, infinite attention to detail, and some knowledge of arithmetic and geometry, to which astronomy was added by Polybius' day (IX, 15):

> In all human undertakings opportuneness is the most important thing, but especially in operations of war. Therefore a general must have at his fingers' tips the season of the summer and winter solstices, the equinoxes and the periods between them, in which the days and nights increase and diminish. For it is by this knowledge alone that he can compute the distance that can be done whether by sea or land. Again, he must understand the sub-divisions of both day and night in order to know at what hour to order the reveille or the march out; for the end cannot be attained unless the beginning be rightly undertaken. As for the periods of the day, they may be observed by the shadows or by the sun's course and the quarter of the heaven in which it has arrived; but it is difficult to do the same for the night unless a man is familiar with the phenomenon of the twelve signs of the Zodiac and their law and order; and this is easy to those who have studied astronomy. ... If ... the nights be cloudy the moon must be watched, since, owing to its size, its light as a general rule is always visible at whatsoever point in the heaven it may be. The hour may be guessed sometimes by observing the time and place of its rising or again of its setting, if you have sufficient acquaintance with this phenomenon to be familiar with the daily variations of its rising. And the law which it too follows admits of being easily observed; for its revolution is limited by the period of one month, which serves as a model to which all subsequent revolutions conform.

To gain the scientific knowledge which endowed him with 'good counsel' and enabled him to exploit circumstances in a rational way, the general should not, however, rely entirely upon personal experience and the skill of his entourage:

> Once more, therefore, those who wish to succeed in military projects and operations must have studied geometry, not with professional completeness but far enough to have a comprehension of proportions and equations. . . . For I do not think that anyone will reasonably object that I

add a great burden to strategy in urging on those who endeavour to acquire it the study of astronomy and geometry. For, while rejecting all that is superfluous in these studies and brought in for show and talk, as well as all idea of enjoining their prosecution beyond the point of practical utility, I am most earnest and eager for all that is essential. It would be strange if those who aim at competence in dancing and flute-playing should study the preparatory sciences of rhythm and harmony (and the same may be said of the pursuits of the palaestra), in the belief that the attainment of these desired skills requires the assistance of the latter; while the students of strategy are to feel aggrieved if they find that they require subsidiary sciences up to a point. That would mean that men practising common and inferior arts are more diligent and energetic than those who resolve to excel in the best and most noble subject. That, no man of sense would admit. (Polybius, IX, 20.)

Military Intelligence

The despatch of special messengers carrying oral or written instructions remained throughout antiquity the safest, most accurate, and often the quickest method of communication. Originally this was a function of amateurs (like the hoplite who, it is said, at the cost of his life was the first to bring the news of the victory of Marathon to Athens). Later it fell to professionals, such as the runner Philonides in Alexander's time, until, finally, in the Roman Empire, regular communication was established through an official post.

The earliest signalling device was the smoke signal: according to legend this was how the Peloponnesians learnt of the fall of Troy. From the fourth century BC, however, more complex methods were devised. One is described by the military writer, Aeneas, reported by Polybius (X, 44–45):

Let those who wish to communicate any matter of pressing importance by fire signals prepare two earthenware vessels of exactly equal size both as to diameter and depth. Let the depth be three cubits, the diameter one. Then prepare corks of a little shorter diameter than that of the vessels;

and in the middle of these corks fix rods divided into equal portions of three fingers' breadth, and let each of these portions be marked with a clearly distinguishable line; and in each let there be written one of the most obvious and universal of those events which occur in war: for instance, in the first 'cavalry have entered the country', in the second 'hoplites', and in the third 'light-armed', in the next 'infantry and cavalry', in another 'ships', in another 'corn', and so on until all the portions have written on them the events which may reasonably be expected to occur in the particular war.

Then carefully pierce both vessels in such a way that the taps shall be exactly equal and carry off the same amount of water. Fill the vessels with water and lay the corks with their rods upon its surface, and set both taps running together. This being done it is evident that if there is perfect equality in every respect between them, both corks will sink exactly in proportion as the water runs away, and both rods will disappear to the same extent into the vessels. When they have been tested and the rate of the discharge of water has been found to be exactly equal in both, then the vessels should be taken respectively to the two places from which the two parties intend to watch for fire signals. As soon as any one of these eventualities which are inscribed upon the rods takes place raise a lighted torch and wait until the signal is answered by a torch from the others: this being raised both parties are to set the taps running together. When the cork and rod on the signalling side has sunk low enough to bring the ring containing the words which give the desired information on a level with the rim of the vessel, a torch is to be raised again. Those on the receiving side are then at once to stop the tap, and to look at the words in the ring of the rod which is on a level with the rim of their vessel. This will be the same as that on the signalling side, assuming everything to be done at the same speed on both sides.

But this procedure, which has much in common with the one Philo of Byzantium recommended at the end of the third century B C, no longer satisfied Polybius.

Now this method [he comments] though introducing a certain improvement in the system of fire signalling, is still wanting in definiteness; for it is evident that it is neither possible to anticipate, or if you could anticipate, to write upon the rod every possible thing that may happen; and therefore when anything unexpected in the chapter of accidents does occur, it is plainly impossible to communicate it by this method. Besides, even such statements that are written on the rods are quite indefinite; for the number of cavalry or infantry that have come, or the particular point in the territory which they have entered, the number of ships or the amount of corn cannot be expressed. For what cannot be known before it happens cannot have an arrangement for expressing it. This is the important point.'

Consequently Polybius recommends the more modern method discovered by Cleoxenus and Democlitus, which he had himself perfected. The letters of the alphabet were divided into five groups, and one could communicate a message by indicating successively flashing signals, the number of the group to which each letter belonged and then its ordinal number within the group (X, 45–47).

Under the Roman Empire a more sophisticated system of signalling made its appearance, which is illustrated on certain panels of Trajan's column. Vegetius (III, 5) makes a brief reference to it: 'Sometimes there are placed on top of the towers of a camp or a town beams which are alternately raised or lowered in order to indicate what is going on.' Indeed, the defence of the frontiers against barbarian invaders depended to a large extent upon the quality of visual communications.

There was a parallel development in the technique of secret messages, for which the ingenuity of the Greeks was a cause of wonderment and produced a whole series of stratagems. The most complicated device, according to Aeneas (XXXI, 17–19) worked as follows:

In a sufficiently large knucklebone bore twenty-four holes, six on each side. Let the holes stand for the twenty-four letters of the [Greek] alphabet, and be careful to remember on which side Alpha comes first and the letters which follow on each side in turn. Then, whenever you wish to communicate any message draw a thread through. For instance, if you wish to express *Aineias* by the drawing through of a thread begin from the side of the knucklebone on which alpha is found, pass the thread through and, skipping the letters succeeding alpha, draw through again when you come to the side where iota is; disregarding the following letters, again pass the thread through where nu happens to be. . . . Continuing in this way, write the rest of the message by passing the thread through the holes in the way in which we have just written the name. Accordingly, there will be a ball of thread wound round the knucklebone and it will be necessary for the one who is to read the message to write on a tablet the letters revealed by the holes. The unthreading takes place in reverse order to that of the threading. But it makes no difference that the letters are written upon the tablet in reverse order, for the message will be read, just the same, although to read what has been written is harder than to 'write' it.

Improvements in the means of communication and of coding facilitated the task of the commander. But they never stimulated the establishment of an autonomous bureaucratic department at headquarters. Improvisation and pragmatism continued to characterise military intelligence and communications.

The Military Magistrates in the Greek Cities

In spite of technical requirements, and no doubt often to their detriment, the Greek cities were for a long time unwilling to entrust army commands to specialists. Any form of authority was held to be an element of political power, not a mere tool. Might of course existed alongside right, and sometimes it was able to force its own law upon the normal organs of government to liberate Mars from his civic chains (especially from the fourth century BC on). When it did so, however, it always sought to justify the exercise of power, as we have seen.

In armies of the aristocratic type, the two aspects of command—political and military, moral and technical—were inextricably fused. In the Homeric poems a 'shepherd of the people' was by definition both a great king and a great captain, for the gods had made a gift to him, at birth, of all the attributes of sovereign power. He distinguished himself both in council and on the battlefield, Odysseus through his guile, Achilles by his impetuosity, and so on. There were no nuances in status.

The emergence of the city and the establishment of the state dislocated the unitary bloc of social functions and so encouraged the emancipation of the military leader. This occurred either through a reduction of the traditionally comprehensive powers of the king as in Sparta; or, more commonly, through the creation of new magistracies, as in Athens. But functional specialisation did not immediately bring specialists into the picture, especially not in the latter type of development. The Athenian army was placed under the command of the polemarch who, together with the other archons, had inherited the royal power. However, in a development which started at the end of the sixth century and was completed between the two Persian wars, this official gradually lost most of his military functions to the *strategoi*. The first power to go was effective command of the armed forces, followed in time even by the nominal command. In Aristotle's day (*Constitution of Athens*, LVIII), the only functions retained by the polemarch were essentially religious in character.

From 501/0 BC the Athenian *strategoi*, formerly attached to the polemarch, constituted a college of ten elected members, one from each so-called tribe. The collegiate system accorded with the principles of democracy recently introduced by Cleisthenes, but it had practical drawbacks which soon had to be overcome with the increasing scale and technicality of military operations. Originally, for example, decisions in the college were taken by majority vote, and supreme command followed a daily rota. But when the Persians landed at Marathon in 490 rotation was abandoned: the other *strategoi* stood down for Miltiades for several days in succession so that he could prepare for battle. The unity and continuity of command were subsequently strengthened in other ways, by the appointment of a single *strategos* to lead an expeditionary force, or as a result of the personal prestige enjoyed by a particular *strategos*. Shortly before 460, the Athenians gave themselves still more freedom of choice by deciding to elect their *strategoi* 'from amongst all', that is to say, independently of the tribal framework.

From the end of the fifth century BC, finally some specialisa-

Familiarity with the sea they will not find an easy acquisition. If you, who have been practising it ever since the Persian invasion, have not yet brought it to perfection, is there any chance of anything considerable being effected by an agricultural, unseafaring population, who will besides be prevented from practising by the constant presence of strong squadrons of observation from Athens? . . . Seamanship, just like anything else, is a matter of art, and will not admit of being taken up occasionally as an occupation for times of leisure; on the contrary it is so exacting as to leave leisure for nothing else. (Thucydides, I, 142, 6–9.)

The Art of Manoeuvre

The principal form of training which was compatible with the traditional ethics of hoplite combat aimed at turning the army into a disciplined and unified force. Hence the art of manoeuvre developed very early in Greece since no discredit was attached to it. Even Socrates approved, little as he thought otherwise of the technical instruction given to the Athenian young of his time by teachers of strategy.

For there is a wide difference between right and wrong disposition of the troops, just as stones, bricks, timber and tiles flung together anyhow are useless, whereas when the materials that neither rot nor decay, that is the stones and tiles, are placed at the bottom and at the top, and the bricks and timber are put together in the middle, as in building, the result is something of great value, a house in fact. (Xenophon, *Memorabilia* III, 1, 7.)

The Spartans, who were the guardians of Greek tradition, were outstanding in the art of arraying and developing hoplite formation. Yet even their efficiency depended upon the simplest principles.

The prevalent opinion [writes their admirer Xenophon, in his *Constitution of the Lacedaemonians* (XI, 5–10)] that the Laconian infantry formation is very complicated is the very reverse of the truth. In the Laconian formation the

165

front rank men are all officers, and each file has all that it requires to make it efficient. The formation is so easy to understand that no one who knows man from man can possibly go wrong. For some have the privilege of leading, and the rest are under orders to follow. Orders to wheel from column into line of battle are given verbally by the second lieutenant acting as a herald and the line is formed either thin or deep by wheeling. Nothing whatever in these movements is difficult to understand.

To be sure, the secret of carrying on in a battle with any troops at hand when the line gets into confusion is not so easy to grasp, except for soldiers trained under the laws of Lycurgus. The Spartans also carry out with perfect ease manoeuvres that instructors in tactics think very difficult. Thus when they march in column, every section of course follows in the rear of the section in front of it. Suppose that, at such a time, an enemy in battle order suddenly makes his appearance in front: the word is passed to the second lieutenant to deploy into line to the left, and so throughout the column until the battle line stands facing the enemy. Or again, if the enemy appears in the rear while they are in this formation, each file countermarches, in order that the best men may always be face to face with the enemy. True the leader is then on the left, but instead of thinking this a disadvantage they regard it as a positive advantage at times. For should the enemy attempt a flanking movement he would try to encircle them, not on the exposed but on the protected side. If, however, it seems better for any reason that the leader should be on the right wings, the left wing wheels, and the army countermarches by ranks until the leader is on the right, and the rear of the column on the left. If, on the other hand, an enemy column appears on the right when they are marching in column, all that they have to do is to order each column to wheel to the right so as to front the enemy like a man-of-war, and thus again the company at the rear of the column is on the right. If again the enemy approaches on the left, they do not allow that either, but either push him back or wheel their companies to the left to face him, and thus the rear of the column finds itself on the left.

ARMY ORGANISATION

Sparta apart, however, it appears to have been no easy task to accustom the soldiers to even the simplest of these manoeuvres. In Xenophon's *Cyropaedia* (II, 2, 6–9) a regimental commander says:

> I assigned the lieutenant his place first, arranged next after him a young recruit, and the rest as I thought proper. Then I took my stand in front of them facing the platoon, and when it seemed to be to be the proper time, I gave the command to go ahead. And that young recruit, mark you, stepped ahead—of the lieutenant, and marched in front of him! When I saw that I said, 'Fellow, what are you doing?' 'I am going ahead as you ordered' said he. 'Well' I said, 'I ordered not only you but all to go ahead.' When he heard this this he turned about to his comrades and said, 'Don't you hear him scolding? He orders us all to go ahead.' Then the men all ran past their lieutenant and came towards me. But when the lieutenant ordered them back to their places they were indignant and said 'Pray, which one are we to obey? For now the one orders us to go ahead and the other will not let us.'
>
> I took this good-naturedly, and when I had got them into position again, I gave instructions that no one of those behind should stir before the one in front led off, but that all should have their attention on this only, to follow the man in front. But when a certain man who was to start for Persia came up and asked me for the letter which I had written home, I bade the lieutenant run and fetch it, for he knew where it had been placed. So he started off, on a run, and that young recruit followed, as he was, with breastplate and sword; and then all fifty, seeing him, ran after. And the men came back bringing the letter.

As the number of men increased and mobility on the field of action grew, it became necessary in the Hellenistic and Roman periods to think up ways of preventing such a shambles by improving the art of manoeuvre. This development is visible in the theorists. From Xenophon through Asclepiodotus to Arrian, the meanings of many technical terms were altered or became more precise, and the number, variety and complexity of formations

167

increased considerably. A good example is the practice of the countermarch, as described in the *Tactical Art* of Asclepiodotus in the first century (X, 13–15):

There are three types of countermarch, the Macedonian, the Laconian and the Cretan or Persian. It is a Macedonian countermarch when the line of file leaders (*lochagoi*) stays where it is while the following ranks, up to the last one, move forward, and then each turns round. . . . It is clear that in a countermarch of this type the phalanx appears to be giving ground and behaving as if it were taking to flight, which emboldens the enemy and has the effect of discouraging those who are taking part in the countermarch. The Laconian countermarch allows the phalanx to occupy a piece of land opposite that involved in the preceding case. For each soldier turns round towards the tail, while the last rank, which we will call klmno, remains where it is; the other ranks fghij and abcde pass round on either side in order to take up their position behind their last rank —obviously in two ways, either file by file or rank by rank—so that the rank fghij takes up a position of FGHIJ and the rank abcde becomes ABCDE. In this way the Laconian countermarch produces upon the enemy the opposite impression from that which is produced by the Macedonian countermarch; for the enemy soldiers appearing in the rear believe that they are dealing with an assault and an attack so that this manoeuvre surprises them and fills them with terror.

As for the countermarch known as Cretan and Persian, it is half way between the other two: for it does not make it possible to occupy either the ground behind the phalanx, as does the Macedonian countermarch, nor the ground situated in front as does the Laconian countermarch: it is upon the same ground that the section leader takes the place of the last man, while the men from behind take the place of the men in front. . . . In this way the countermarch does not change the position of the phalanx, which is very useful to us when the ground situated in front and behind it are less advantageous.

Weapon Training

It goes without saying that a certain expertise in the use of the lance, the sword and the shield was always demanded of the hoplites. But it was only at the end of the fifth century BC that specialists in military swordsmanship appeared in Greece, and at first they were regarded with some suspicion. Supporters and adversaries of this new discipline confront each other in Plato's early dialogue, the *Laches*, in which the Athenian general Nicias, portrayed as a man of progress, says:

> This accomplishment will be of some benefit also in actual battle, when it comes to fighting in line with a number of other men; but its greatest advantage will be felt when the ranks are broken and you find you must fight man to man, either in pursuing someone who is trying to beat off your attack, or in retreating yourself and beating off the attack of another. Whoever possesses this accomplishment could come to no harm so long as he had but one to deal with. . . . (181E–182B).

Laches, also a general, replies in these words:

> . . . not one of these experts in arms has ever yet distinguished himself in war. . . . Whether it be an accomplishment, and one of but little use, or not an accomplishment but only supposed and pretended to be such, it is not worth the trouble of learning it. For indeed I hold that if a man who was cowardly believed he possessed it, his only gain would be in rashness, which would make his true nature the more conspicuous, while if he were brave, people would be on the look-out for even the slightest mistake on his part, and he would incur much grievous slander (183C–184B).

All the same, from the fourth century the use of arms played a more important part in military training. In the Hellenistic armies, other forms of specialised training arose for the light infantrymen, with an oval shield and a small sword, for the archers, the javelin throwers and those manning the catapults. However, this progress had little effect upon the heavy infantry, if we may draw an inference from the comparatively few relevant words of command mentioned by late Greek writers on tactics, in particular Asclepiodotus (XII, 11: 'Lower arms!', 'Arms at the ready!', 'Shoulder arms!').

It was only in the Roman legions, particularly after the professionalisation in the early first century BC that the ordinary soldier was systematically trained for single combat. The basic techniques, hurling the javelin and sword fighting, had long been familiar in Rome, among the gladiators who were taught in specialised schools. The chronicler Valerius Maximus (II, 3, 2), writes as follows about the training methods introduced into the Roman army by Marius in 105 BC:

> The theory of the use of arms was only taught to the soldiers from the time of the consulate of P. Rutilius, the colleague of Cn. Mallius. No general before him had done this, but he summoned masters of the gladiators from Cn. Aurelius Scaurus' school and introduced to our legions a more accurate method of parrying and dealing blows. He thus produced a combination of courage and skill in such a way that the one reinforced the other, with courage supplementing skill with all its zeal, and skill teaching courage how to safeguard itself.

This innovation naturally did not fail to trouble the traditionalists, who were still expressing their displeasure at the beginning of the second century AD, for example, Pliny the Younger, in his *Panegyric* (XII, 4-5):

> Such were the great generals of the past, bred in the homes of Fabricius, Scipio and Camillus; if they have a lesser claim upon my admiration it is because in their day a man could be inspired by keen rivalry with his betters. But now that interest in arms is displayed in spectacle instead of a discipline, when exercises are no longer directed by a veteran crowned by the mural or civic crown, but by some petty Greek trainer, it is good to find one single man to delight in the traditions and valour of our fathers, who can strive with none but himself for rival, press on with his own example before him, and since he is to wield authority alone, will prove that he alone is worthy.

Nevertheless the military instructors did in fact take over, with adaptations, the training techniques evolved in the schools for gladiators.

> This is how the ancients trained their recruits (as can be seen from their books). They made round shields of wickerwork, like wattle, so that the wattle weighed twice as much as a normal shield. Likewise, instead of swords they gave the recruits staves which were twice the weight. They used these in practice against stakes, not only in the morning but also in the afternoon. For practice with stakes is as useful to soldiers as to gladiators. Nobody in the arena or on the battlefield has ever proved to be invincible in combat without having assiduously practised the stake exercise. Each recruit would drive his stake into the ground so that it was firm and stood six feet above the ground. He then practised against this stake, as if against an adversary, armed with his wattle shield and with his stave in lieu of a sword; at times he would strike it a blow as if he were aiming at the head or face, sometimes he would attack its sides, and sometimes he would try to slice at the hamstrings or legs, leaping backwards, attacking, cleaving the stake in two with might and main, with all his fighting skill, as if the stake were a real adversary. In this exercise care was taken that the recruit should lunge so that he landed his blows without leaving any part of his body unprotected (Vegetius I, 11).

The recruit then began the second stage of his training (called *armatura*, as in the schools for gladiators). Now he learnt to use the sword, the javelin, and sometimes the bow and the sling, perhaps even to throw stones and leaded darts. His instruction was then considered to be complete. To quote Vegetius again (I, 13):

> All actual battles offer proof that soldiers who have completed their training fight better than the others. . . . The ancients preserved their training procedures so jealously that they gave double rations to the masters-of-arms, while soldiers who had profited little from this military preparation were obliged to accept barley instead of wheat, and

were given their ration only after they demonstrated, in a public trial, in the presence of the prefect of the legion, the tribunes and other superior officers, that they had mastered all the branches of the military art. Indeed there is nothing more stable, more prosperous, more glorious than a state which abounds in trained soldiers. For it is not the splendour of uniforms nor the abundance of gold, silver and precious stones which make us respected or sought out by our enemies: they can only be forced to submit through terror.

Military Training

Under the Roman Empire, young recruits were given a privileged status to enable them to undergo their training properly. Circumstances permitting, efforts were made to keep them out of the battle line for a certain period, before they were brigaded with the veterans. This had seldom been the case previously: recruits were either acclimatised by simulated battles at the beginning of a campaign or they were simply given more responsibilities as they acquired more combat experience.

There is a twofold reason why formal training had been either neglected or left to chance: the rudimentary expertise required of soldiers and the numerous opportunities in civilian life for initiation into the profession of arms, either through hunting (which did not differ substantially from war except in its objectives) or, especially among the Greeks, through the athletic contests and dances which played such a large part in education and in the religious festivals. Day in day out, in effect, the future hoplites raced, jumped and threw the javelin in the gymnasia, wrestled and boxed in the palaestra, dreaming of a victory in the regular competitions organised by the cities and the great sanctuaries, and at the same time acquiring the basic qualities of the hoplite. In the Hellenistic period the programme of the gymnasia and palaestrae expanded to include new exercises, such as fencing, archery and even the firing of catapults, and thus continued to satisfy the essential needs of military training.

There was also a military side to some dances linked with religious celebration. In the most famous, the so-called Pyrrhic, warriors danced in the nude to the accompaniment of a flute, but there were others, too, such as those performed at a festival by the mercenaries of Xenophon's *Anabasis* (VI, 1, 5–11), according to the traditions of their native districts.

> After they had made libations and sung the paean, two Thracians rose up first and began to dance in full armour to the music of a flute, leaping high and lightly and using their sabres; finally one struck the other, as everybody thought, and the second man fell, in a rather skilful way. . . .
>
> After this some Aenians and Magnesians arose and danced under arms the so-called *carpaea*. The manner of the dance was this: a man is mowing and driving a yoke of oxen, his arms laid at one side, and he turns about frequently as one in fear; a robber approaches; as soon as the sower sees him coming, he snatches up his arms, goes to meet him and fights with him to save his oxen. The two men do all this in rhythm to the music of the flute. . . .
>
> After this a Mysian came in carrying a light shield in each hand, and at one moment in his dance he would go through a pantomime as though two men were arrayed against him, again he would use his shields as though against one antagonist and again he would whirl and throw somersaults while holding the shields in his hands, so that the spectacle was a fine one. Lastly he danced the Persian dance, clashing his shields together and crouching down and then rising up again; and all this he did keeping time to the music of the flute.
>
> After him the Mantineans and some of the other Arcadians arose, arrayed in the finest arms and accoutrements they could command, and marched in time to the accompaniment of a flute playing the martial rhythm and sang the paean and danced, just as the Arcadians do in their festal processions in honour of the gods.

Still other religious manifestations, liked the armed processions and the ritual battles derived from initiation practices, contributed in one form or another to the apprenticeship of the young. But the most important factor was the spirit of emulation which made them seize spontaneously upon every opportunity to develop their warlike qualities. No one doubted that it was these that gave substance to the liberty of the citizen and guaranteed that autonomy of the city. Military skill was thus to a large extent acquired through a process of osmosis and imitation. Even so, most Greek cities did not believe that the state was entirely exempt from taking a hand in military training. Citizens subject to call-up were required to participate in periodical reviews, which enabled the officials to check on the arms and deportment of their troops.

As for the adolescents, in the years preceding their incorporation into the army, they had to undergo a special regimen, which varied from city to city and which was in principle the adaptation for educational purposes of an initiation rite. At Sparta, where the individual was strictly subordinated to the community, young boys left the family circle at the early age of seven, though they did not embark on their apprenticeship as citizens and soldiers until they were twelve. They were then divided into 'herds' (*agelai*) under the supervision of instructors and whipbearers, under the eye of their elders with whom they were individually bound by emotional, pederastic ties. They were trained for the tough life of the camp, sleeping on beds of leaves, sharing the famous Spartan gruel, and wearing the same light-weight garment in all weathers. At eighteen, they were subject to new tests, including the ritual combat round the altar of Artemis Orthia. A little later they entered a period of retreat (the *crypteia*), during which they led a rough and dangerous life on the frontiers, devoted, in particular, to hunting down helots. They were finally recognised as full soldiers and citizens at the age of twenty-four.

Similar training principles were to be found in the Cretan cities, where they gave rise to comparable, though less developed, institutions. Young Cretans of good family were also divided into age groups and 'herds'. However, personal ties between lover and beloved, and the patronage by local aristocrats of individual 'herds' weakened the state's monopoly of education in Crete more than in Sparta.

The Athenian *ephebeia* presents a slightly different impression of this type of institution, which must have existed in one form or another in all Greek cities. Unfortunately, we have a fairly precise idea of the *ephebeia* only at a relatively late date, from the last third of the fourth century BC. By that time its original

174

organisation and aims had been obliterated or altered by the development of the city, and had come to reflect current political preoccupations. Each young Athenian of hoplite status, having been entered in his deme register and having undergone the examination which assured his citizenship status and his physical condition, was called to serve in the ranks of the *ephebes* between the ages of eighteen and twenty. They were placed under the control of various officials elected by the people: there were a director, ten preceptors—one from each tribe—with the rather vague duty of 'looking after the *ephebes*', two instructors, a master-of-arms, a master of archery, a master of the javelin, and a master of catapults. The first year began with a tour of the sanctuaries, possibly the occasion when they swore the following oath, which by the fourth century had become archaic in its vocabulary and in the choice of divine witnesses:

> I will not dishonour the sacred arms; I will not abandon my comrades in battle; I will defend both the sacred and the secular (rules of the community) and I will hand on to my juniors a fatherland in no way diminished, but larger and more powerful so far as it is within my power and with the aid of all. I will obey the magistrates, the established laws and those which may be introduced; if any man seeks to overthrow them I will oppose him with all my strength and with the aid of all. I will venerate the cults of my ancestors. I take as witnesses to this oath the gods, Aglauros, Hestia, Enyo, Enyalios, Ares and Athena Areia, Zeus, Thallo, Auxo, Hegemone, Heracles, the boundary-stones of the country, the wheat, the barley, the vines, the olive-trees, the fig-trees.*

The *ephebes* were then divided into two contingents and installed as garrisons in two fortresses of the Piraeus, at Munychia and at Acte. The second year began with a review before the assembly of the people in the theatre of Dionysus, and

* The text of the oath is taken from a stele, found in the Attic deme of Acharnae, with a pediment on which is represented in relief the defensive armour of a hoplite; see M. N. Tod, *A Selection of Greek Historical Inscriptions* II (Oxford, 1948) no. 204. It is not certain whether the ephebes swore the oath at the beginning of their two-year period or at the end.

with a solemn conferring of arms. Then the *ephebes* went off to guard the territory, patrolling the frontiers or stationed in rural fortresses.

This system had apparently been a response to the national shock of the Athenian defeat by Philip of Macedon at Chaeronea in 338 BC. But it soon began to change and to lose some of its military and political significance as the city was forced steadily to reduce its political and military pretensions. We can observe how, even before 250 BC, the *ephebeia* was being converted into a cultural institution and began to admit rich foreigners and to exclude poor citizens. By the time of the Roman Empire it was no more than a civic manifestation of pomp and luxury. The *ephebes,* writes the orator Philostratus in his *Life of the Sophists* (IV, 22), once used to swear in the sanctuary of Aglauros to die for their country and to take up arms, whereas nowadays they swear only to celebrate the feasts of Bacchus for their country and to take on the *thyrsus* without wearing a helmet, just like women.

In sum, throughout its evolution, the Athenian *ephebeia* had in different contexts assumed different functions, first social, then military and finally cultural, but it never lost its religious character. As late as the reform introduced after Chaeronea, it still retained archaic traits reminiscent of the initiation rites of primitive societies. The offering of hair and the wearing of a black *chlamys* symbolised the passage from childhood to adulthood. The compulsory and official nature of the institution, as well as its religious aspects, bound it intimately with the life of the community. Yet, since the *ephebe* lived on the frontiers and was barred (except in certain cases) from testifying in court, he occupied during his initiation a marginal position with regard to the city, spatially and juridically.

The Italian world also retained well into the historical period, many traces of a primitive division of the young into age-classes. But initiation was never transformed into an institution for military training as among the Greeks. In Italy, the associations of young men, both before and after their reform by Augustus, performed only a cultural and religious role, with little military significance. Their function was theatrical rather than competitive, a function of exhibition or representation of the community, not of its defence.

Military Discipline

Discipline, the final, essential condition for an army to function properly is in the first place the product of its organisation and that, in its turn, depends on the command structure and on the army's place within the social system. At any given moment, discipline may also be influenced by fortuitous factors, but they should always be assessed as a function of the army's receptivity. As the quintessence of the military spirit, discipline expresses a necessarily unstable equilibrium among all the forces, internal and external, which effect the behaviour of the soldier.

In the aristocratic armies, whose principle of coherence was social rather than truly military, order appears to have been ensured simply by an affirmation of lines of precedence. Odysseus at Troy had no need of military regulations in order to dress down the impudent Thersites for his defeatism. He 'berated him with harsh words', saying:

> 'Thersites of reckless speech, clear-voiced talker though you are, refrain and be not minded to strive singlehandedly against kings. For I believe that there is no viler mortal than you amongst all those who came to the walls of Ilium with the sons of Atreus. Therefore it would be good that you take not the names of kings in your mouth as you prate, to cast reproaches upon them and to watch for our return home. In no way do we know clearly as yet how these things are to be, whether it be for good or ill that we, sons of the Achaeans, shall return. You continually revile Atreus' son Agamemnon, shepherd of the host, because the Danaan warriors give him many gifts; whereas you babble on with insults. I will tell you, and what I say will come to pass, if I find you again playing the fool, as you are now doing, may the head of Odysseus rest no more upon his shoulders nor may I any more be called the father of Telemachus if I do not take you, strip off your raiment, the cloak and tunic that cover your nakedness and send you wailing to the swift ships, beaten forth from the place of assembly with shameful blows.'

So spoke Odysseus and with his sceptre smote his back and shoulders; and Thersites cowered and large tears fell from him; stung by pain and with helpless looks, he wiped away a tear. But the Achaeans, vexed at heart though they were, broke into a merry laugh. (*Iliad*, II, 246–270).

This strict paternalism, also manifest at the beginnings of Roman history, in the forms of paternal authority and client-ship, was superseded by the rule of law when the city-state made its appearance. The most important law in our context fixed a penalty of death, exile or loss of civic rights for the most serious and most obvious crime which any citizen could commit on the battlefield, namely abandoning his post and therefore creating a breach in the compact formation of the phalanx. However, the rule of law also protected the soldier-citizen against arbitrary actions. The army, an extension and detachment of the people, did not enjoy legal immunity. This is why the heaviest sanctions could be applied only by recognised representatives of the popular will, whether the army assembly or the popular assembly or a military magistrate.

Thus protected by their paramount status as citizens, soldiers were often fairly casual about discipline. They had little to fear from their commanders for venial faults for, in a sense, they themselves had elected their leaders. Even mutiny, which could erupt when discontent was general, was never wholly without legitimacy; like any normal decision reached by the civic body as a whole—and in a certain sense even more pertinently—mutiny was an expression of the popular will. This is the fundamental reason underlying the 'indiscipline' in classical Greek armies and their inability to comply with the most elementary security precautions, especially when booty was being collected. The situation was similar in the Roman Republic although the sense of state was more firmly established and the army was better structured. We should beware of being misled by a few examples of ferocious discipline ascribed to the earlier Romans, in all likelihood exceptions which later imperial writers emphasised for purposes of edification.

From the Hellenistic period onwards, loyalty to the leader replaced respect for the laws as the ultimate basis for military discipline. This change is clearly seen in the oaths sworn by the combatants. In Rome, for example, originally there were an oath of allegiance to the laws (*sacramentum*), possibly inspired by Samnite customs, which consecrated the soldiers in a magico-legal sense to the service of the state, and an oath of mutual solidarity (*iusiurandum*) to reinforce the personal relationships within the army. In 216 BC the latter was replaced by a supplementary oath of loyalty to the magistrates in command of the armies.

> After completing the enrolment, the consuls waited a few days for the contingents furnished by the Latins and allies to come in. Then a new departure was made: the soldiers were sworn in by the military tribunes. Up to that day there had only been the military oath binding the men to assemble at the bidding of the consuls and not to disband until they received orders to do so. It had also been the custom, among the soldiers, when the infantry were formed into companies of one hundred and the cavalry into troops of ten, for all the men in each company or troop to take a voluntary oath to each other that they would not leave their comrades for fear or for flight, and that they would not quit the ranks save to fetch or pick up a weapon, to strike an enemy or to save a comrade. This voluntary covenant was now changed into a formal oath taken before the tribunes (Livy XXII, 38, 1–5).

The commander's personal hold over his soldiers was thus strengthened increasingly. The Roman emperors made extensive use of this type of oath to ensure the loyalty of their troops. In the end, they also demanded it of civilians. Concurrently the sense of hierarchy was strengthened on the practical plane, the coercive apparatus on the legal plane, and, on the ideological plane, the glorification of *Disciplina militaris,* which acquired altars in the reign of Septimius Severus, at the very moment when it was beginning to be severely attacked.

Once again, war is revealed to have been an active agent, not merely the passive product, in the historical evolution of ancient societies. In order to ensure their maintenance and efficient functioning, the armies found that they had to create their own mode of organisation, more or less integrated within the traditional framework of the civil communities, which could end in the substitution of a bureaucracy for the 'natural' hierarchical system.

Conclusion

However 'objective' a historian tries to be in a general survey such as we have just completed, the account is necessarily an interpretation. It is therefore proper, in conclusion, to attempt an explicit statement of the role of war in the organisation and development of ancient societies. For this purpose the Greek and Roman witnesses are insufficient in themselves. The modern historian has the duty and responsibility of progressing beyond the historical awareness of the ancient writers.

A further difficulty arises, as I also noted in my introduction, from the current state of war studies in general. The explanations offered for these historical 'accidents' called wars continue to oscillate between two extremes in historical-political thinking. There is an analogy in popular explanations of road accidents: on the one hand, man's imprudence and his congenital taste for danger are denounced, on the other hand, blame is placed on the fortuitous combination of circumstances which caused the crash. Both kinds of explanation, often produced at the same time, explain everything and therefore explain nothing, neither the frequency of accidents nor their severity nor the form they take. A historical generalisation cannot be constructed merely by amassing a series of facts (however accurate they may be), without taking account of the psychological motivations behind the facts, the social structures in which they are embedded, and the totality of the historical development.

Historians of antiquity therefore lack the detailed studies and partial syntheses essential for an overall appreciation of the military phenomenon. The reflections which follow are frankly schematic and incomplete.

The Causes of War

In antiquity, as in modern times, every war erupted out of an unstable complex of rational and emotional motivations, real or imaginary, conscious or unconscious. Hence no typology can definitively establish homogeneous, 'chemically pure' categories.

At a first glance, the wars of antiquity appear to be conflicts over sovereignty, confrontations between antagonistic groups seeking to increase or to preserve their collective power. On this abstract level, any war can be labelled a political phenomenon. However, if one restricts the political category to actions which are deliberately and specifically connected with the existence of the group as such, the field becomes narrowed to those conflicts which had as their principal, if not sole, objective, the development of political structures; whether internal, in the consolidation of the power of the state, or external, in a drive to incorporate other communities. Examples would be the 'ritual' wars through which the integration of the younger age-classes into the group of adults was consecrated; the 'monarchical' wars waged to increase the prestige of a sovereign; the 'agonistic' wars inspired by the spirit of competition between cities; the 'strategic' wars which realised on a local level a more general programme of imperial expansion.

Alongside these essentially political wars with which we may include the markedly ideological 'sacred' wars, there were others, economic in character, aimed at the immediate satisfaction of the community's material needs. Such were the wars of plunder which were common in the accounts of the origins of Rome; or the so-called 'commercial' wars for control of the centres of 'strategic' supplies (minerals, wheat, slaves), rather than for control of market outlets.

Most often, however, political and economic interests appear to be inextricably linked, one or the other predominant according to whether the historian is looking at the beginning or the end, the causes or the consequences, of a military operation. Hence the temptation to ascribe greater importance to one or the other, either by taking the view that economic advantages fell to the victor as a sort of bonus, without their actually seeking them, or else by dismissing the political motive as mere pretexts. Both approaches fail to apprehend war not as a means of action, but rather as a mode of existence. In contrast, proper consideration of the underlying social organisation reveals that the ambiguity of the military phenomenon is altogether natural.

For a human community to be in a position to make war, the first condition is that satisfaction of its immediate needs leaves a residue of vital energy available for military activity. On the economic level, the forces of production must be sufficiently developed to create a surplus of resources for investment in non-productive (or not immediately productive) activities, among the most important of which is war.

That level had already been attained in Greece before the middle of the second millennium, in Italy by the end of that millennium, in other words, by the beginning of the historical period in both regions. The division of labour had already given rise to a process of social differentiation reinforced by relationships based on exploitation. Given the low productivity of human labour, only the use of force, either to seize the product or to subject the producer, could ensure a surplus. Both societies were still in a predatory stage in the history of economic development. There was no question of exploiting the producer only indirectly, by buying his labour through a voluntary wage-contract. A kind of generalised servitude locked in an extremely close network of personal obligations characterises the Greek world down to the Homeric age, the Roman to the early Republic. Only a small elite escaped.

These conditions severely restricted the growth of the forces of production, and the very survival of the communities was jeopardised. The difficulties were then overcome by some communities, through an increasing exploitation of less developed peoples, either by the reduction to servitude of native peoples in a block (such as the Laconian helots), or by the importation of barbarians who were reduced to slavery as individuals. The economic and social tensions within the privileged communities were thus relieved. Their own members could now all be granted the full measure of freedom; their internal solidarity and homogeneity were strengthened in opposition to the servile masses; finally they transformed themselves into city-states, communities of citizens within a clearly defined juridical framework and a more sophisticated state structure. But because the blossoming of these sharply defined political minorities was determined by the exploitation of outsiders, by a fatal logic they also began to exploit each other despite their basic solidarity and cultural ties. Different procedures were required from those

CONCLUSION

which could be applied to 'barbarians'. When more was involved than a periodic raid to seize resources, account had to be taken of the political situation of the adversary and a status preserved for him more honourable and less harsh than servitude. There were two possible solutions: either tribute could be levied or the territory could be annexed, depending on tradition and historical circumstances.

It was therefore the same impulse which led ancient states both to introduce chattel slavery into their midst and to seek to dominate one another. The two modes of exploitation differed in degree, not in kind. They belonged to a single system of appropriation by coercion. That is why most conflicts between organised states were simultaneously economic and political in character: exploitation and subjection were synonymous. In the ancient world power and wealth were not independent notions; each fed on the other. It was therefore not from hypocrisy, conscious or subconscious, that power was used to seize wealth or that wealth was seized in order to enhance power. The language was always the same in passing from politics to economics, that of Force, mother of Authority and Property.

With this perspective it is easier to understand both the frequency and the scale of military operations in antiquity, to grasp why ancient history was so heavily stamped with the vicissitudes of war. There are two reasons. When internal contradictions, class antagonisms, were still relatively weak, the impact of external differences (between one tribe and another, one people and another) stood out in sharp relief and played a decisive role in the historical dialectic. On the other hand, weak commercial relations could not easily be reconstructed once destroyed. The consequence was that in antiquity, war put in question the whole social system at is various levels (economic, political, even religious), and thus had a profound effect upon the course of ancient history. A conquering state did not always wish nor was it always able to impose its own mode of organisation. But war, through its own brutal decisions, altered the relations between communities from the outside; its consequences were not merely to create a new political order, it bore directly on the foundations of civilisation itself.

WAR IN THE ANCIENT WORLD

War and Politics

Warfare, like colonisation, aimed only to ensure the development of the communities by outer expansion: this was the principal mode of development possible in antiquity, given the state of the forces of production. War therefore tended, on the one hand, to 'freeze' social relationships by providing a diversion that checked the deepening of internal antagonism. But it also had its own requirements, which affected the internal development of society, so that, on the other hand, war tended to burst the limits of a system it was designed to perpetuate and, in the end, to help destroy that system.

The impact of war was particularly clear in the political field. Most historians of antiquity are agreed that small tribal communities were the point of departure for the evolution which gradually led to the formation of states (city-states and kingdoms). Their internal cohesion was based upon real or fictitious kinship. In times of peace, the 'natural' order, strongly structured though scarcely at all hierarchical, perpetuated itself with little change from generation to generation, for the power of tradition was enough to ensure the survival of the elementary groups composing the community. In times of war, however, circumstances imposed a new order as the communities who found themselves united in a common struggle needed a more centralised organisation which could give more opportunity for technical competence. The new military hierarchy was originally restricted to the duration of a conflict, but eventually it became more or less permanent, until life appointments and even hereditary posts made their appearance. Duties were transformed into posts, burdens into profitable benefices. Created in order to serve the community, military power finally held the community in its service. A fact became a right, force gave birth to law in the name of the higher interests of an expanded community which had become increasingly differentiated both economically and socially.

Just as it contributed to the dissolution of the 'natural' order of the pre-state communities and to the creation of a truly political order, war then continued to affect the development of new structures. By the fourth century BC in Greece, war freed itself from city-state control even before it sealed their fate under Macedonian armed might. The Roman Republic which had given fuller recognition to military necessities, suffered the same fate, but at the hands of its own armies. Political power passed to individual conquerors, Hellenistic kings and Roman emperors. And when the society of the late Empire, suffering from a profound internal crisis and threatened by the growing pressure of the barbarians, did away with the traditional institutions, once again it was the military power, that inexhaustible source of sovereignty, that assumed the task of regenerating imperial power.

Similarly, war sometimes compelled the ancients to exceed the natural limits of their economy, by removing some of the obstacles to growth imposed by the social relations of production and the corresponding ideology. Thus war could stimulate a spectacular and rapid development in technology by the practical application of theoretical research, in a world in prey to a kind of technological block, which normally prevented mechanisation of the means of production. It required the challenge of external danger to liberate man's inventive genius from the constricting prejudices against technological progress, and then only in this limited sector. The very existence of the community had to be at stake. The perfection of siege engines from the fourth century BC is the best testimony, along with the simultaneous advancement of the military engineer in status and social prestige. One might also mention the concentration of manpower and the division of labour in the military workshops of the late Empire, in some ways foreshadowing modern manufacture. More generally one may even ask whether it was not behind the original development of a class of artisans. The existence of fundamental links between the worlds of the warrior and the craftsman (originally called, in Greek, a *demiurgos*, a worker in the service of the people), would then explain why both these categories appear to have enjoyed certain fiscal privileges in the Mycenaean kingdom of Pylos.

Ancient war also made its contribution to the creation and extension of a monetary economy, thus stimulating the growth of production for trade, with all that meant for the course of social evolution. Before coinage became a genuinely economic instrument, subject to the demands of commerce, its original essential function was to define relationships between men, not

185

between commodities. It facilitated and regularised the financial operations necessitated by the creation of states. For one thing, coinage made possible prompt mobilisation of community resources on a large scale in times of war. When mercenary armies came into use, in particular, their employer had to have a relatively large quantity of coins at his disposal at the right moment, even if, as was frequently the case, the mint had to produce a special issue for the purpose.

In most of Greece such coins were usually indistinguishable from those normally minted. That mercenaries were the recipients can be inferred only if there is some modification in the type, if a particular series appears to have been unusually abundant or if the hoards discovered in modern times are peculiarly located. If, furthermore, such a sign is linked chronologically with documentary evidence of massive employment of mercenaries—by no means always the case—the inference is that much stronger. Occasionally, however, especially on the periphery of the Greek world, the coins themselves reveal the identity of the first recipients. For instance, in fourth century BC Asia Minor and Egypt, satraps and native rulers used coin types and standards visibly adapted to the recruitment of troops internationally. Or, early in the same century, the Carthaginians issued specially marked tetradrachmas, on Greek models, for their mercenaries in Sicily: one type carried the head of Arethusa, a Syracusan device, on the obverse, and on the reverse a Carthaginian device (a horse's head) and a date palm to help Greeks identify the source,* and the words, in Punic characters, 'men of the camp' (*am machanat*).

All in all, the link between the mercenary system and monetary policy in the Greek cities seems to be so close that some scholars have explained the invention of coinage in Lydia or Ionia about 625 BC in this way. However, it seems better not to take so exclusive a view and to acknowledge the payment of soldiers as the basic, though not the sole budgetary requirement that underlay this invention.

It is anyway evident that war contributed more than the desire for gain to the refinement of the instruments of exchange

---

* The point is a pun on 'Phoenician' or 'Punic': the Greek word for 'palm' is *phoinix*.

in antiquity. The earliest financial manipulations seem often to have been carried out as 'stratagems' imposed by military requirements. One example from our chief source, the second book of the pseudo-Aristotelian *Oeconomica* must suffice. The author is describing (II, 2, 23a) how fiduciary money was introduced in military camps in the fourth century BC, as promissory notes to be honoured after victory: 'Timotheus of Athens during his campaign against Olynthus was short of silver, and issued to his men a copper coinage instead. On their complaining, he told them that all the merchants and retailers would accept it in lieu of silver. But he instructed the merchants to buy with the copper they received, in turn, such produce of the land as was for sale, as well as any booty brought to them; whatever copper remained on their hands he would exchange for silver.'

Once coinage had been invented for use by the state, and had become more widespread and efficient in the state's service, especially in the discharge of military responsibilities, it was obviously used for commercial purposes as well. But a long time passed, much longer than is usually allowed, before commercial purpose became the overriding consideration in the state's monetary policies. That had not yet occurred, for instance, by the end of the Roman Republic. As one expert has recently shown:

> During the Republic, for which a fairly close chronology and a very accurate estimate of the relative size of issues are now available, the volume of coinage struck fluctuated as the number of legions in the field went up or down and as other state expenses rose and fell. For example, the only large issue of the 70s BC is to be dated 74 BC and related to the help sent to Pompey in Spain.*

Both economically and politically, in sum, war asserted its particular claims which, depending on circumstances, either confirmed or contradicted the traditional principles on which society was organised. Since in ancient communities the law of growth and development was based on the use of force, while

---

* M. H. Crawford, 'Money and Exchange in the Roman World', *Journal of Roman Studies*, 60 (1970), p. 46; see also his 'War and Finance', *Ibid*, 54 (1964), pp. 29–32.

the political framework and economic basis were too weak to bear the pressures of expansion, war tended to impose its own structural compulsions. This explains the permanent trend towards militarisation in these societies, one which we ourselves have not yet altogether overcome.

> For man to raise himself in order to organise his societies upon other bases would mean for him a long, painful and precarious victory over himself, the experience of which alone can teach him how necessary it is. A truism perhaps, but a truism which, if it is ignored, may have momentous consequences.*

* A. Aymard, 'Esprit militaire et administration hellénistique', *Revue des Etudes Anciennes*, 55 (1953), p. 145; reprinted in his *Etudes d'histoire ancienne* (Paris, 1967), p. 467.

Select Bibliography

GENERAL WORKS

H. Delbrück, *Geschichte der Kriegskunst im Rahmen der politieschen Geschichte*, I, *Das Alterthum* (1900; new ed. by K. Christ, 1964).

H. Droysen, 'Heerwesen und Kriegführung der Griechen', in K. F. Hermann, *Lehrbuch der griechischen Antiquitäten*, II² (1889).

W. Rüstow and H. Köchly, *Geschichte des griechischen Kriegswesens von der ältesten Zeit bis auf Pyrrhos* (1852).

J. Kromayer and G. Veith, *Heerwesen und Kriegführung der Griechen und Römer*, in W. Otto, *Handbuch der Altertumswissenschaft*, IV 3² (1928): the most recent and most useful work, with full bibliography, to be supplemented (until 1939) by the articles in the *Jahresbericht über die Fortschritte der klassischen Altertumswissenshaft* by F. Lammert for Greece, vol. 274 (1941) 1–114, and by C. Blümlein for Rome, 201 (1925) 1–64; 218 (1928) 69–100; 248 (1935) 148–99; 274 (1941) 115–51. For the years after 1939 comprehensive bibliographies have yet to be assembled.

SPECIAL TOPICS

A. Momigliano, 'Some Observations on Causes of War in Ancient Historiography', in *Acta Congressus Madvigiani*, vol. 1 (1958) 199–211, reprinted in his *Studies in Historiography* (London: Weidenfeld, 1966), ch. 7.

Greece:

F. E. Adcock, *The Greek and Macedonian Art of War* (University of California Press, 1957).

P. A. L. Greenhalgh, *Early Greek Warfare* (Cambridge University Press, 1973).

J. K. Anderson, *Military Theory and Practice in the Age of Xenophon* (University of California Press, 1970).

J. F. C. Fuller, *The Generalship of Alexander the Great* (London: Eyre; New York: Funk and Wagnalls, 1958).

W. K. Pritchett, *The Greek State at War* (2 vols, University of California Press, 1971–74).

W. W. Tarn, *Hellenistic Military and Naval Developments* (New York: Biblo and Tanner, 1930).

J. P. Vernant, ed., *Problèmes de la guerre en Grèce ancienne* (Paris, 1968).

Rome:

F. E. Adcock, *The Roman Art of War under the Republic* (Cambridge: Heffer; New York: Barnes and Noble, 1960).

R. MacMullen, *Soldier and Civilian in the Later Roman Empire* (Harvard University Press, 1967).

H. M. D. Parker, *The Roman Legions* (1928), re-edited by G. R. Watson (New York: Barnes and Noble, 1967).

G. R. Watson, *The Roman Soldier* (London: Thames and Hudson, 1969).

G. Webster, *The Roman Imperial Army of the First and Second Centuries A.D.* (London: Black, 1969).

J. P. Brisson (ed.), *Problèmes de la guerre à Rome* (Paris, 1969).

CHAPTER 1.

H. A. Ormerod, *Piracy in the Ancient World* (Liverpool University Press, 1924).

H. J. Dell, 'The Origin and Nature of Illyrian Piracy', *Historia*, 16 (1967), 344–58.

R. MacMullen, *Enemies of the Roman Order* (Oxford University Press: Harvard University Press, 1967) 192–241, 255–68.

F. Jacoby, 'Patrios Nomos', *Journal of Hellenic Studies*, 64 (1944) 37–66.

D. W. Bradeen, 'The Athenian Casualty Lists', *Classical Quarterly*, 63 (1969) 145–59.

W. C. West, 'The Trophies of the Persian Wars', *Classical Philology*, 64 (1969) 7–19.

H. S. Versnel, *Triumphus* (1970).

A. Alföldi, 'Hasta-Summa imperii, the Spear as Embodiment of Sovereignty in Rome', *American Journal of Archaeology*, 63 (1959) 1–27.

P. Ducrey, *Le traitement des prisonniers de guerre dans la Grèce antique* (Paris, 1968).

On ancient diplomacy, the rather antiquated work of C. Phillipson, *The International Law and Custom of Ancient Greece and Rome* (London: Macmillan, 1911) and the collection of texts, *Die Verträge der griechisch-römischen Welt*, II, ed. H. Bengtson (1962), and III, ed. H. H. Schmitt (1969).

SELECT BIBLIOGRAPHY

CHAPTER 2.

Y. Garlan, 'Les esclaves grecs en temps de guerre', in *Actes du colloque d'histoire sociale de Besançon 1970* (*1972*) 29–62.

J. F. Gilliam 'Enrolment in the Roman Imperial Army', *Eos*, 48 (1957) 207–16.

R. W. Davies, 'Joining the Roman Army', *Bönner Jahrbücher*, 169 (1969) 208–32.

N. Wood, 'Xenophon's Theory of Leadership', *Classica et Medievalia*, 25 (1964) 33–66.

J. Roy, 'Xenophon's Evidence for the Anabasis', *Athenaeum*, 46 (1968) 37–46.

H. W. Parke, *Greek Mercenary Soldiers, from the Earliest Times to the Battle of Ipsus* (Oxford University Press, 1933).

G. T. Griffith, *The Mercenaries of the Hellenistic World* (Cambridge University Press, 1935).

P. A. Brunt, *Italian Manpower 225 B.C.–A.D. 14* (Oxford University Press, 1971).

J. K. Anderson, *Ancient Greek Horsemanship* (1961); 'Homeric, British and Cyrenaic Chariots', *American Journal of Archaeology*, 69 (1965) 349–52.

M. W. Frederiksen, 'Campanian Cavalry', *Dialoghi di Archeologia*, 2 (1968) 3–31.

On the earliest relations between the cavalry and the Roman patricians, A. Alföldi, *Entretiens sur l'antiquité classique*, 13 (1966) 223–90, and various articles of A. Momigliano collected in his *Quarto contributo . . .* (1969) 273–499.

J. W. Eadie, 'The Development of Roman Mailed Cavalry', *Journal of Roman Studies*, 57 (1967) 161–73.

A. M. Snodgrass, *Early Greek Armour and Weapons* (Edinburgh University Press, 1964; Cornell University Press, 1967); *Arms and Armour of the Greeks* (London: Thames and Hudson; New York: Aldine, 1967).

A. E. Wardman, 'Tactics and Tradition of the Persian Wars', *Historia*, 8 (1959) 49–60.

J. G. P. Best, *Thracian Peltasts and their Influence on Greek Warfare* (1969).

R. D. Milns, 'Philip II and the Hypaspists', *Historia*, 16 (1967) 509–12; 'The Hypaspists of Alexander III—Some Problems', *Historia*, 20 (1971) 186–95.

191

G. V. Sumner, 'The Legion and the Centuriate Organization', *Journal of Roman Studies*, 60 (1970) 67–78.

M. J. V. Bell, 'Tactical Reforms in the Roman Republican Army', *Historia*, 14 (1965) 404–22.

Y. Garlan, *Recherches de poliorcétique grecque* (Paris, 1974).

E. W. Marsden, *Greek and Roman Artillery* (Oxford University Press, 1969–71).

F. E. Winter, *Greek Fortifications* (University of Toronto Press, 1971).

J. S. Morrison and R. T. Williams, *Greek Oared Ships, 900–322 B.C.* (Cambridge University Press, 1968).

L. Casson, *Ships and Seamanship in the Ancient World* (Princeton University Press, 1971).

J. H. Thiel, *Studies on the History of Roman Sea-Power in Republican Times* (1964); *A History of Roman Sea-Power before the Second Punic War* (1954).

C. G. Starr, *The Roman Imperial Navy* (new ed., Cambridge: Heffer, 1960).

A. Momigliano, 'Sea-Power in Greek Thought' and 'Terra marique', in his *Secondo contributo* . . . (1960) 57–67, 431–46.

CHAPTER 3.

C. W. Fornara, 'The Athenian Board of Generals from 501–404' *Historia, Einzelschrift* 16 (1971).

E. Birley, *Roman Britain and the Roman Army* (1953).

C. Pélékidis, *Histoire de l'éphébie athénienne* (1962).

F. S. Lear, *Treason in Roman and Germanic Law* (University of Texas Press, 1965).

C. E. Brand, *Roman Military Law* (University of Texas Press, 1968)

CHAPTER 4.

M. I. Finley, 'Technical Innovation and Economic Progress in the Ancient World', *Economic History Review*, 2nd ser., 18 (1965) 29–45.

H. W. Pleket, 'Technology and Society in the Graeco-Roman World', *Acta Historiae Neerlandica*, 2 (1967) 1–25.

E. S. G. Robinson and M. J. Price, 'An Emergency Coinage of Timotheos', *Numismatic Chronicle*, 7th ser., 7 (1967) 1–6.

W. E. Thompson, 'The Functions of the Emergency Coinages in the Peloponnesian War', *Mnemosyne*, 4th ser., 19 (1966) 337–43.

For comparison, see:

SELECT BIBLIOGRAPHY

A. Andreski, *Military Organisation and Society* (University of California Press, 1954).

G. Bouthoul, *Traité de sociologie: les guerres. Eléments de polémologie* (1951).

M. R. Davie, *The Evolution of War: a Study of Its Role in Early Societies* (New York: Kennikat, 1929).

R. Numelin, *The Beginnings of Diplomacy* (Connecticut: Kerry, Lawrence, 1950).

A. J. Toynbee, *War and Civilization* (Oxford University Press, 1950).

H. H. Turney High, *Primitive War* (University of South Carolina Press, 1949).

A. Vagts, *A History of Militarism* (New York: Free Press, 1937).

Q. Wright, *A Study of War* (2 vols., University of Chicago Press, 1942).

INDEX

195

INDEX